When God Comes Knocking

When God Comes Knocking

Sandy Tovray

Northwest Publishing, Inc.
Salt Lake City, Utah

When God Comes Knocking

For information address: Northwest Publishing, Inc.
6906 South 300 West, Salt Lake City, Utah 84047
BK 8-3-94
G. E. Bloomsburg

PRINTING HISTORY
First Printing 1994

ISBN: 1-56901-373-x

NPI books are published by Northwest Publishing, Incorporated, 6906 South 300 West, Salt Lake City, Utah 84047.

PRINTED IN THE UNITED STATES OF AMERICA.
10 9 8 7 6 5 4 3 2 1

I proudly dedicate this book to Rayna,
a true hero, and to Tovah,
because there is more than one kind of hero.

Foreword

Sandy Tovray here chronicles her family's journey along a seemingly solitary path, beginning with the shocking discovery that her younger daughter had a serious medical problem. With clarity, candor, and wit, she shares her anxiety, hopes, and fears as the diagnosis unfolds, as treatment options are weighed, and as life and death decisions are confronted. Her courage and resourcefulness shine forth in these pages, mirroring the courage, love, and inspiration she drew from her husband and daughters as they traveled that road together.

Other participants in the drama portrayed in these pages make only cameo appearances; the central drama plays out in the life of this family. While the participation of other family members, of people in the medical profession, and of teachers and friends are generally presented anonymously, only two physicians, a rabbi, and a custodian are mentioned specifically by name. This dramatically underscores the fact that dealing with an illness is something which, in the final analysis, involves primarily the ill person, her family, and those friends who are involved on a day-to-day basis with all aspects of their lives.

We, as physicians, can evaluate the clinical findings and data of a particular case, offer opinions about what course of action might be pursued, and discuss which, if any, options might be preferable. Our advice will be based on our knowledge, personal experience, and understanding of possible side effects and complications of the various treatments available. Ultimately, the patient and/or the family must make the final decision about which course to pursue. Once the decision is made, we draw upon all resources available to us to help in implementing that decision. We must always remember that whatever treatment we carry out, the patient will live, or sometimes die, as a consequence. Our participation will always be that of an outsider, playing an almost incidental role in the larger drama engulfing the patient and her family. We must always remind ourselves that while this case may be one of many in which we are involved, it belongs uniquely to the patient and is the most important case in the world to her. Patients may recognize intellectually, and perhaps emotionally, our need to allocate time and energy to our various responsibilities. We should never, however, allow them to think that we consider their problem to be less important to us than anyone else's.

Ms. Tovray's observations on the evaluation, planning, and treatment process carried out in our department (Radiation Oncology, Massachusetts General Hospital, Boston, Massachusetts) are also illuminating. I frequently observe patients arriving at the treatment area, or see them in the waiting area prior to their visit with the doctor or their appointment in the treatment room. A few of them are known to me: the illness which brings them there, the potential for successful treatment, and even cure of their condition, what side effects the treatment may produce, and what their future course might be. These factors in other patients can be guessed at from some external circumstances: the head coverings, an obvious lesion in the head and neck area, their waiting room attire, and the treatment room to which they proceed when called. In all cases, I can only observe and, perhaps, participate in the treatment process. Even then, I am only an observer, not an "experiencer."

It is an unfortunate reality that most radiation therapy facilities are located below grade, or, as we term our treatment area, on "the lower level." This is to avoid calling it "the basement," with whatever associations that term might have. The author avoids the lower level euphemism, forthrightly describing the MGH department as being in the basement. She insightfully shares the depression she felt at having to "press the down button on the elevator," and asks plaintively "Aren't our lives down enough?" Unfortunately, economics dictate that modern high energy treatment facilities be located below grade to avoid the cost of supporting and building large concrete or steel walls which would effectively confine radiation from our therapy units to the treatment room.

Rayna received her treatment at our current proton beam treatment facility, the Harvard Cyclotron Laboratory on the Harvard University Campus in Cambridge. This venerable accelerator, built as a research tool almost half a century ago and largely obsolete as a research instrument, has been used by MGH for patient treatments for over four decades. The Cyclotron Laboratory has many endearing qualities. Not the least of these is that both treatment rooms there are located on the street level, effectively shielded by thick concrete walls or by large mounds of earth heaped up against already thick walls, which prevent radiation from reaching the outside world. There are no windows in the treatment rooms, but patients and their families know that they have not descended to a lower level, allowing them to understand, at least subconsciously, that getting treated does not require them to "press the down button on the elevator," which may itself have a positive effect on the treatment experience.

Alas, reality intrudes, and "progress" occurs. A new treatment facility on the MGH campus will replace the antiquated Harvard Cyclotron before the century ends. This will allow treatment techniques which cannot be carried out at the current facility and significantly increase patient treatment capacity. However, the new treatment facilities will be located below grade in something which we will call the "treatment level." We are planning to have a skylight project into the main corridor of the treatment level, preserving at least a glimpse of the outside world. The reality, however, is that our new treatment facilities will be in what Ms. Tovray would undoubtedly recognize as "the basement."

I have often reflected on the feeling patients must have when they are left alone in the treatment room as the radiation therapists who do the treatment each day and whatever family members may have accompanied them into the room depart, abandoning them to the rays from the machine. Usually, a massive steel door closes, totally isolating them until the treatment is completed. Each treatment room in our current department at MGH does indeed have a "large ominous door" which must be shut before the beam can be turned on. These doors are electronically wired so that incomplete closure or inadvertent opening activates a circuit termed a "safety interlock," designed to protect persons in the room or those outside the room from radiation exposure. There are no doors to the treatment rooms themselves at the Harvard Cyclotron, at least to my perception. Rather, both rooms have large concrete mazes which block the radiation. Security is provided by interlocks on a gate to one room and by a normal door with wire-reinforced glass windows leading into the area in which Rayna was treated. Even this standard door, such as might be seen leading into a warehouse or industrial facility, impressed Ms. Tovray as a "large ominous door," reminding us again that our perceptions, and indeed reality, are not always what the patient and her family perceive.

A standard "history and physical exam," such as might be written by an attending physician upon admission of a patient to the hospital, would require one or two pages to adequately describe Rayna's story in stark medical terms. A third or fourth-year medical student's notes might take four or five pages to tell the same story. The author's moving account of her daughter's experience poignantly reminds us that our dry medical prose provides only the sketchiest outline of the true drama of anguish, joy, anxiety, sorrow, triumph, and sometimes defeat, which accompanies every patient's illness. She has "fleshed out," both literally and figuratively, the emotional roller coasters of the patient's life prior to, during, and after our encounter with her. Through better understanding of what patients and their families go through, and how this affects their lives, we can become better prepared to deal with our patients, and in the process, become better physicians.

My experience has been largely limited to treating patients with benign or malignant tumors, rather than conditions like Rayna's. Her treatment was indeed unique, although other patients have since been treated in a similar manner. Only time will tell if her treatment succeeded in preventing recurrent difficulties, or whether it may cause others to develop. Once our prescribed treatment course has been completed, we can only hope, and sometimes pray, that it will have been successful, and that no bad effects will result from our treatment.

Ms. Tovray alludes briefly to the sense of guilt which assailed her at learning the diagnosis wondering "what had I done?" The sense of responsibility that patients or family members feel for obtaining a prompt diagnosis and proper treatment when an illness develops comes through in the text, as well as the tremendous stress placed upon parents, spouses, or children by a medical diagnosis and by the need to seek and obtain appropriate treatment. Anxieties persist even after the treatment has been concluded; questions like "what will the scan show?" or "will there be a recurrence?" or "did they get it all?" cannot all be answered. Clearly, a sense of confidence and optimism on our part can help the patient to deal with these and other questions which arise after the relatively intense interaction accompanying the treatment is over, and the follow-up phase begins.

Ms. Tovray also weaves Rayna's sister Tovah into the tale by recounting events and milestones in her other daughter's life and detailing the role that the big sister played in helping Rayna and her parents cope with the reality of her illness. The father, too, emerges as a central player in this drama. As the curtain falls, we have been privileged to have shared an intimate and prolonged insight into how this family's love strengthened and sustained them in dealing with the illness of one member. It is most gratifying to learn that their love was strengthened by this ordeal, and that life has gone on after its completion. For sharing this story with us, we can only be grateful to Ms. Tovray.

I am deeply honored to have been asked to comment on the manuscript which Rayna's diagnosis, treatment, and, indeed her life, have inspired. Ms. Tovray is a superb storyteller. One would hope that a sequel might be written, allowing us to share the rest of Rayna's life and that of her family.

John E. Munzenrider, M.D.
Associate Professor
Department of Radiation Oncology
Massachusetts General Hospital

Acting Clinical Director
MGH Proton Therapy Program
Harvard Cyclotron Laboratory

Acknowledgment

In Rayna's twelve years of life, there have been numerous people who have touched her life, made it better in one way or another.

Although each and every person was, and still is, an integral part of Rayna's story, only a few were mentioned in this book. To all the others, all so special, I thank you for all you have done to enhance the quality of Rayna's life—physically, emotionally, academically, spiritually. So many special people: friends, relatives, doctors, nurses, secretaries, custodians, educators, camp counselors, occupational therapists, physical therapists, psychologists, people, anyone who ever smiled at Rayna, ever inquired about her health, her well-being, who touched and continues to touch Rayna's life in one way or another.

You've "risen to the occasion," "rallied to the cause," and, although the battle is not yet won, the enemy has seen defeat and is retreating and, with a little bit of luck, perseverance and prayers, will continue to do so—forever.

And thank you, Allyn, for your expertise in smoothing out some of the medical jargon still baffling to me, and for your true understanding of my need to write this book.

Thank you also to Dr. John Munzenrider for contributing the foreword to this book. Your expertise in medicine is only surpassed by your compassion and understanding for your fellow man.

And, of course, a thank you beyond what words can express on paper to the two wonders of my life, Tovah and Rayna. They give me support, inspiration, and courage.

I could never have written this book without all the support of the people mentioned above. As people helped Rayna, they helped me as well; for Rayna's tears are my tears and Rayna's laughter is my laughter. Thanks for helping to put the laughter back in my life. Rayna has an expression: "If you smile at someone, someone will smile back at you." Because of Rayna, there are a lot of people smiling in this world.

Introduction

I remember sitting at birth class watching a film on cesarean birth, thinking to myself, I don't know why I am watching this; it isn't going to happen to me. A few months later, I gave birth to my first child, by cesarean. I learned something very valuable then: never say never.

I'm not the first mother to have a child with a medical problem, and unfortunately, probably not the last. To know Rayna is to love Rayna and to love Rayna is to know Rayna. Not original thoughts, just correct ones.

I am not a psychologist, nor an expert on child rearing, just a mother deeply in love with her daughters. Some of my thoughts may seem universal, others rather unique. No matter which, they are all thoughts from the heart. If this book can offer some encouragement, some strength, at least one "non-sleepless" night, and some genuine hope when that last straw seems to have been broken, then I'll know I did something wonderful.

Many valuable lessons were learned in the last decade of my life as I faced the ordeal of Rayna's illness. I try to live my life by some of these lessons. One dominant theme has to do with control. I learned that lack of control doesn't preclude action; it doesn't mandate ineffectuality; it doesn't mean surrendering all that you can do; it doesn't mean giving up hope. Don't ever give up hope; cling to it with a fierceness, and treasure its potential.

If you bought this book or borrowed it from the library, I thank you for taking the time to read it and hear my story. If someone bought this book for you as a present, the person must think very highly of you and I thank that person as well.

When thinking about this book, I pondered many titles, having much difficulty determining a suitable one. Perhaps I wanted a few words or a little expression to say it all: all the fears, the tears, the anguish, hopes, frustrations, etc. How can one small title say all that? What could describe all the months and years of dealing with our situation? I thought of "Rayna's Story," "Rayna's Hopes," "One Child, Many Problems," "Never Say Never," and then something happened. This story is about Rayna, yes, but it is also a story about a family, about all people, about life.

Halfway through the writing of this book, an incident occurred that made me think of the title. My older daughter Tovah was having a medical problem, that luckily turned out not to be serious. But for a few nightmarish nights, there was concern that her symptoms represented something quite serious. Again, just as when Rayna was diagnosed, a series of tests was ordered, and once again, I found myself in that state of complete panic, so familiar by this time. As I hoped and prayed that nothing serious was wrong, I questioned many things. One question kept popping up in my head—"Can this be happening to Tovah as well; can God be knocking twice?" The results of her testing showed that this incident was of no serious consequence. As I cried with relief, I knew that I had found the title for this book.

Chapter One

SO MUCH FOR THE GAME

December, 1984

I went to New York with my husband, Allyn, for a weekend away: a weekend of fun; a weekend when the titles of Mommy and Daddy were temporarily replaced by Sandy and Allyn; a weekend to rediscover my husband away from Legos, away from gourmet lunches of grilled cheese sandwiches and chocolate milk, followed by the ultimate in entertainment, *Sesame Street*. I had never really left the girls, and packing even a small suitcase, I felt as if I was leaving my whole world behind me. And I was. After all, Tovah, age five, and Rayna, age three, were my whole world, and they were staying home.

"Come on, Sandy," shouted Allyn. "We'll miss the plane. It's only two days. Enough good-byes."

But are there ever enough good-byes? How do you say good-bye to your whole world, even for forty-eight hours? I hopped in the cab without looking back, for I knew if I looked back, I would see a little girl in pigtails, with her toothless smile, waving away at me. Next to her would be a smaller girl, clutching her favorite doll, smiling brightly at the window. And I would tell the cab driver to forget the whole thing. So I looked straight ahead and told myself, rather brainwashed, that I deserved a weekend away with my husband. Just because I have two children doesn't mean I gave up the title of wife. Brainwashing is obviously not one of my fortes. The cab had hardly reached the main road when the first of many a kleenex was extracted from my pocketbook. How do other parents do it so easily? How do they pick themselves up and leave their children so easily? I can't believe that they are any less loving parents. Maybe because this was my first time. That's it. I had never left them like this before. It would get easier.

The cab turned onto another road, even closer to the airport, even further away from my daughters. Why doesn't he turn around? Can't he hear my heart pounding? Can't he look in his rearview mirror, see the pain on my face—the worry that I don't know how to leave my family? Does he have children? Does he have two adorable little girls who love to play house, pretend what it will like to be the mommy? Do they cook at a pretend stove with pretend food, then cuddle up to him and open his mouth, making him eat the pretend lasagna as he exclaims, "Yum!" in an exaggerated voice, smacking his lips, swallowing the pretend feast, then grabbing his girls and tickling them and giggling with them? Has he ever gone away and left his family? Why does he insist on driving me to the airport when I don't really want to go? And look at Allyn. How can he sit there so calmly reading over the latest in his professional journal, the airplane tickets as his bookmark? No, it wouldn't get any easier to leave them next time. Besides, I wasn't even sure there would ever be a next time.

Allyn is an oral surgeon, and he had a meeting in New York City. I would fill the time that he was busy with meetings by shopping and working on my writing. I am an aspiring screenplay writer. I would also spend the weekend doing my absolute best not to stop at every phone booth, long distance calling card ready for action.

I went to New York with a heavy heart, but I was reassured they were in the capable hands of my cousin, Barbara, a first grade teacher. I knew she would be wonderful with them. After all, if she can take care of twenty-three six-year-olds for six hours a day, she can certainly take care of two children for about fifty hours. She'll be the one to remind them to brush their teeth, read them their story, hear about the fun time they had at Cindi's birthday party, the one to hug them good-night.

I went to New York and I came home from New York, and life has never been the same and never will be. You see, that weekend a discovery was first made, not the kind of discovery you get excited about like the one in 1492 or one by Thomas Edison, not a discovery that would change the whole world, just my world, and Rayna's. This was the discovery that Rayna had an illness, a horrible, terrible illness.

We returned home, refreshed, rejuvenated, and grateful. We even took separate planes as some parents believe in. We are cautious parents. We are overly cautious parents. We know we can't put our children in plastic bubbles and roll them through life protecting them against all of life's adversities. In reality, we don't do that, but in our hearts, we wish we could.

Allyn is one of those people who is always one step ahead of himself, looking for ways to avoid danger, conflict, anything that will impede a happy, safe life for his children. But the one thing that even Allyn can't do, nor I, nor any human being for that matter, is change the things that are uncontrollable, and that's what Rayna's illness was—something completely, utterly out of anyone's control—at least on this earth. Nothing I said, nothing I ever did, nothing I ever ate, nothing I ever wrote about or even dreamed about; nothing could have prevented this illness. If that was the case, then why did I feel so guilty? I think my guilt was just as inherent as Rayna's illness.

She was born with a genetic abnormality, some blood vessels that didn't form in the proper way. And for three and one-half years, they just inhabited her head in this twisted-up fashion, unobtrusive, "minding their own business," not making their presence known, until one day they just let go and started to bleed, and bleed, and bleed, ever so slowly, right in front of our eyes, until one day, she couldn't use her right hand, so she used her left hand. And that's what Barbara noticed, and that's where the story begins, and that's when one chapter of my life was closed and another opened. I had the best intentions with my pregnancy—no caffeine, no alcohol, not even a sip of wine. The best intentions, the best efforts—uncontrollable results.

The doctors believed that the blood vessels had been slowly leaking for about six months, with no apparent effects, nothing noticeable, until the day, well, you know what day that was.

Rayna was sitting with a toy on her right side, twisting her body around to the right so she could use her left hand to pick it up. Barbara stared wide-eyed at this occurrence, this unusual way to pick up a toy. Barbara kept observing this behavior, curious as to why she favored her left hand. It wasn't even just favoring. She was clearly going out of her way to avoid using the right hand. Rayna wasn't complaining of any pain in her hand or arm, nor anything else, no headache, no pain, no whining, no crying—just having a fun weekend with her cousin, enjoying life—sitting with a time bomb in her head.

Upon our arrival, loaded with gifts, hugs, and kisses, I knew the best part of my getaway weekend was my return home and feeling those delicious hugs and wet kisses from my two favorite people in the whole wide world. I had left my whole world behind me, and now I was safely reunited with it. Yes, the best part of my trip to New York was hugging my children in Massachusetts.

We hardly got in the door, distributed our gifts, kisses, hugs, and enough love to—well, there's never enough love—before Barbara pulled me aside.

"Rayna doesn't use her right hand," she cautiously whispered.

"I know," I whispered back, but for what reason, I couldn't fathom.

"We think she'll be a lefty." Not dismissing a concern, stating a fact. "Cousin Ben is a lefty, and Aunt Lil."

But Barbara wasn't satisfied with this answer and told me to watch her for a few minutes. So, we all sat down to dinner, and the girls ate with relish, happy and content that the family was back together. I went from staring at Rayna to making eye contact with Barbara, giving her nonverbal signals that I now understood her concern, to knowing that if I took one mouthful of food, it would be one more mouthful that my body would keep. It felt like that last moment when the beautiful setting sun, that sought-out red ball, lights up the sky in an array of bold colors that can camouflage any problem in the world, then finally sinks beyond the horizon, and we return to reality. Something told me at that moment, I didn't want to face reality.

I look back on that night, remember the sinking feeling I immediately had, the realization that there was something wrong. This was not an observation to be dismissed casually. It's amazing how vulnerable we all are in this world. How, in a single second, the world can change for us. How, the earth can feel so safe, and the next moment, we can be devastated by an earthquake; the world can be at peace, then plagued by war; one minute we are enjoying a meal in a restaurant, the next, a victim of some lunacy and a sniper attack; one minute we are the parents of a healthy child, the next in fear for her life.

I kept telling myself nothing was wrong with my child, I was being silly to panic, to jump to conclusions. I always push the panic button before the elevator has reached that floor.

There was nothing wrong with my beautiful baby and that was that. Now finish your meal—fat chance.

Later, in the privacy of our darkened bedroom, I relayed all of this to Allyn, and "Mr. Red Flags Alert" himself assured me there was nothing wrong. I spoke in a whisper just the way Barbara had. The children were asleep; a low voice would have been sufficient in not awakening them. Was I whispering because I felt that this would keep it at bay, that if I didn't actually say the words out loud, then they couldn't be true? I had this fantasized misconception that saying horrible thoughts out loud would validate them; whispering would make this horrible, ominous feeling disappear.

"Barbara thinks there is something wrong with Rayna," I whispered. There, I said it, but it can't be true, because I whispered it. Besides it can't be true because there can't be anything wrong with Rayna. And I got just the answer I wanted.

"She was probably just fooling around, having fun with Barbara because we were away."

"Great!" Problem solved à la Allyn.

In a few days she was due for a checkup anyhow, and we would definitely share this observance with the doctor—share this observance—just like we shared the observance of that first exciting step, her first words, her first sentences, the first letter of the alphabet she could write in awkward, spindly fashion. So, okay, this observance wasn't quite like that, a little different, but everything would be okay. It had to be. Allyn is usually the one to push all the panic buttons and he calmly said she was okay. So, she was okay.

The sleep I so desperately needed would not come. I searched my mind for any clues, any indications that all was not right. I remembered a few weeks ago her nursery school teacher had voiced her concern that Rayna was not walking the stairs by alternating feet, but rather, placing both feet on the same stair before moving on. She had also noticed that Rayna seemed to be the last one to run across a gym floor and felt that perhaps Rayna needed some more encouragement in participating in physical activities. I remember panic washing over me; that feeling when you hear something isn't picture perfect about your perfect child; the feeling similar to the one I felt now, since Barbara's announcement.

After her teacher's comment, the next time Rayna was on the stairs, I demonstrated the alternating sequence to her, and immediately, she followed suit and alternated her feet. I also enrolled her in a gym class as suggested. It was to start in a few weeks and then both observations would be conquered, problems erased. She alternated the stairs and she would increase her physical activity. I was appreciative of the keen observations and "on top of the situation" capabilities of the nursery school teacher, thankful that nothing was wrong with my child and looking forward to the gym class.

That gym class never materialized for Rayna.

I finally drifted off to sleep temporarily contented that at least my children were safely tucked in next to our bedroom instead of two hundred miles away.

My "peaceful sleep" was disturbed in the early hours of the morning as Allyn shook me. He had a glazed look in his eyes.

"Good morning, darling" was replaced with "There's definitely something wrong with her, call Dr. Mandell." What had changed from the setting sun to the rising sun? He said she was okay. I went to bed believing that, praying that. Allyn said he had been up for hours, thinking.

Thinking of how every time he would wash her hair, she would never turn her head to the right and would laugh. We thought it was a game, "three-year -oldness." He reminded me of how every time I would take off her turtleneck, I used to get it stuck. I always believed it was her beautiful thick hair. In retrospect, I realize she was fisting her hand underneath as I did it. Clues, blatant clues; what kind of parents were we? Later on, psychologists reassured us that these signs weren't as blatant as we were blaming ourselves for; that part of Rayna's strength was compensation, overcompensation; somewhat reassuring.

I walked into the pediatrician's office apprehensive. Other

mothers were there cooing with their babies, or, for the older ones, shouting universal declarations of "Share the toy with that nice boy, Ben," making appointments, getting throat culture reports. Were any mothers sitting there with their hearts pounding, their mouths dry, wondering if they were going to find out something more than Susie has an ear infection or Carl has to have a measles shot? I wanted results like that. I imagined a scenario.

"I'm pleased to tell you, Sandy and Allyn, that this is a normal part of development. They stop using their right hand completely for three months. It's a psychological test that all three-year-olds give their parents to see if they can tolerate stress in raising children."

"Thank you, Dr. Mandell. Now, we'll go back to worrying about normal things. Have a nice day."

It only took two minutes for the pediatrician to perform some quick, basic neurological tests before telling us that Rayna needed to see a neurologist. I walked out of the pediatrician's office never to be the same again. Where was my pat on the back that everything was okay, my prescription for medicine to make it go away? That's what I wanted, not a little piece of paper with the phone number of a neurologist. That was one name I'd definitely have to whisper. Saying it out loud was too scary, carried too much baggage with it.

"Could something really be wrong with this beautiful, seemingly healthy three-year-old, so bright, so full of life and hope?" I didn't want to answer my own question.

Rayna has such a zest for life; she claps her hands in glee with such excitement when I bring home the first batch of strawberries for the season. She marvels at a spectacular sunset, relishes the melodious sounds of a beautiful song, gasps in ecstasy over delights others may just take for granted. She definitely gives validity to the expression "stop and smell the roses." No, I will wake up and this nightmarish feeling of doom will disappear. But, morning after morning came. The sun rose, the sun set. Nothing made any of this disappear.

We saw a neurologist immediately. After an extensive

clinical examination, the doctor looked us square in the eye and told us four things. Yes, something was clearly wrong with Rayna. A CAT scan was imperative. She appeared, in the doctor's initial opinion, to have a mild case of cerebral palsy, "CP." She would take the possibility of a brain tumor and put that unthinkable (yet it was all that permeated my mind) possibility as last on the list.

Cerebral palsy? Rayna? Cerebral palsy was something you read about in books, watched television movies-of-the-week about, read true stories about in women's magazines, and showered those stricken with it, with sympathy. It was not something your three-year-old daughter, who only yesterday you were thanking God was born normal, could be afflicted with.

What did I do wrong? Why her? Why anyone? Why sickness in the world? And why a child, a poor innocent child, only familiar with the external world for about forty months? I tried to calm myself, but I suppose that's like trying to calm down a claustrophobic stuck in an elevator. The CAT scan was in two days and then I would know. I didn't know which was worse, the agony of waiting and not knowing, or the agony of knowing.

In between fits of anxiety came calm moments when I rationally and intelligently thought the situation out by putting it in perspective, by playing the "It could always be worse" game. When I really concentrated and told myself at least it's not a tumor, at least it's not cancer, and put the whole thing into perspective, a momentary calm would wash itself over me. So, when my heart would race, when I would read a book for an hour and realize I hadn't even turned the page, when I just couldn't stand the agony of the unknown, I would play the game.

"Okay," I would scream into my brain, "so it's CP, so at least you know, at least it's not anything worse, at least it's not a tumor." Hey, this game really helps. Two days later, on an unseasonably warm, sixty degree December day, a CAT scan revealed, that Rayna, my precious child, had a brain tumor. So much for the game.

Chapter Two

SHIVERING WITH THE CHILLS

Rayna was sitting with a time bomb in her head as questions exploded in mine—questions that I wish I had the answer to and yet didn't want to know.

So now what? What next? How do we all go on from here? How we do we try to put our lives back together or live with the fragmented pieces of what is there? How do you try to repair a priceless glass vase smashed into a thousand pieces?

The supportive response that infiltrated our lives as the news spread was overwhelming. The first to appear unannounced at our doorstep was Dr. Mandell. He entered the house, somber face, open, nurturing arms, with words of encouragement, sympathy, and sage advice. One of his main concerns, beyond the immediate problem, the obvious medical consequences of the result of the

CAT scan, was to help us deal with the girls, what to say, what questions to expect, and what answers would be appropriate.

One of these concerns was directed toward Tovah, making her aware that she "didn't cause Rayna's illness," "she can't catch Rayna's illness," and thirdly, "nothing she ever wished or thought made this happen to Rayna." These were helpful words of wisdom, and his presence gave us a sense of security, even for a fleeting moment, until he left.

Rayna just went with the flow. We'd give her minimal explanations of what was happening to her so she wouldn't be frightened. Any questions asked would get an answer; we wouldn't hold back the truth, just give her information in child dosages. Tovah, as well, was the recipient of these doses. Her needs were many at this time, with much concern for her sister. She was well aware that the household was different. For one thing, the phone rang more times than a charity phone-a-thon. I never realized what an integral part of the community I was until this happened. I didn't have to stand in the middle of town with a megaphone announcing that my three-year-old was just diagnosed with a brain tumor.

"Hear ye, hear ye." No, that was replaced with human curiosity, gossip experts, and genuine concern for a tragedy.

The phone would ring, the mailman would deliver letters.

"Dear Sandy and Allyn...sorry to hear about...anything we can do...you must...don't hesitate..."

Some friends wanted to make a supper chain, each taking a different night to bring over a dinner, so we didn't have to think about it. Thanking them profusely for their selflessness and devoted friendship, I declined. They had done this for me a year ago, when my mother died. The memories of that were too fresh. No, I didn't want supper. No one had died.

And I was no longer just Sandy Tovray. I now had a new identity. I was transformed into Sandy Tovray, "the mother of the one with the brain tumor." It's amazing how we categorize people by their past, present, and even future events: "He's the one who's going to be the new principal." "You know Sally Stone, the one with the twins." The divorced one, the owner of, the new tenant, the CEO, the head of, the fired one, the one who, the one with, the one that....

Our identities in life become attached to who we are, what we eat, where we work, etc., and the more noted we are in the public eye, the more attached our identities are. And because I was noted then, talked about, sympathized, I now was "the mother of the one with the brain tumor."

One day, as I was walking out of the school after dropping the girls off, I was approached by an acquaintance.

"Sandy, oh my God, how are you? How's Rayna? I want to hear all about her. Now I know she had an appointment last Thursday and did okay." All this said in one breath. I guess my megaphone could stay in the back of the closet.

The next medical step was an arteriogram. This would determine if the lesion was due to abnormal blood vessels in the brain. So there was a possibility that it wasn't a malignant tumor, that the mass was blood, some sort of arterio-venous malformation. Yes, a glimmer of hope, a light in the tunnel, although still a bleak story.

If I thought I felt a sense of abandonment and loss when I left the girls for a weekend in New York, nothing could come close to the feeling I experienced when I had to drop Tovah off at a friend's house to give her breakfast and a ride to kindergarten in order for us to get to the hospital early. I clung to her as I delivered her to my friend. I knew she was in good hands with a warm and compassionate person, but I couldn't help feeling a major void. But, no problem was going to get solved standing on the doorsteps on this cold December morning, trying to sweep my anxieties under her doormat. With shaking hands, I stooped down to Tovah's level, stared into those big brown eyes, and assured her that we were all going to be fine. She shook her little head up and down, and I believed her. She believed all was going to be well, and I was going to catch her enthusiasm and inspiration.

We checked into day surgery for an eleven o'clock appointment for the arteriogram. I looked around the room as other surgical candidates sat on the floor playing with wooden puzzles or television character puppets, as their parents sat in chairs watching them, or sleeping, or attempting to read. The children seemed unaffected, unaware of the impending agenda for the day, just happy, carefree children playing, waiting for their names to be called to take them to their surgery. The children played, the parents fretted. One could almost forget why they were even in this waiting room. Rayna's name was called. No more fantasizing of where I was and for what purpose.

Rayna's procedure entailed giving her intravenous sedation, then connecting catheters through the groin to the brain, and reading what the results were. We arrived to friendly nurses, reassuring and caring. They showed us where to lock up our coats and personal belongings and where to wait with Rayna before they took her to surgery, before they took my baby away from us and for a few hours put her in the hands of others to take care of her. That feeling of abandonment I experienced when dropping Tovah off was upon me again. Seeing your child being wheeled off to surgery, with tubes in her arms, so small under that white sheet, so vulnerable, so fragile, so alone despite a team of health professionals hovering over her. Although we were only a few feet away from one another, that feeling of separation felt worse to me than if we had been placed at opposite ends of the earth.

Unfortunately, the case before Rayna's had complications, so Rayna's case wasn't started until midafternoon. We were told once Rayna went in, we could wait in the parent's lounge, a place which, we discovered, housed lots of worried eyes, wringing hands, frightened tears. These all belonged to other parents waiting for their beloved offspring to be returned to them from surgery.

So, we sat in the waiting room with undrunk cups of coffee getting cold and magazines on our laps with pretty pictures and unturned pages. And we waited. At last, we were told it was over, but that Rayna had needed more sedation than anticipated, and due to the late hour of the day, it would be best to keep her overnight.

Keep her overnight? Not go home to her bed, her stuffed animals, dolls, Mickey Mouse night light, Cinderella slippers, Tovah? With much anguish, we quickly decided that I would stay with Rayna and Allyn would go home to be with Tovah. Two parents, two children, two problems solved—at least the sleeping arrangement problem. One step at a time. Baby steps. Baby steps to cover big areas.

We could meet her in the recovery room in about ten minutes. Allyn had to leave; he had made an appointment with another doctor for some more opinions. He would return later with Tovah to say good-night to us. I went to the locker, retrieved my coat, gave Rayna's personal belongings to the orderly who would take them to her room, threw my coat on a chair in the waiting room, and ran to be reunited with Rayna in the recovery room. I entered the recovery room as Rayna was being wheeled in.

She looked so beautiful, so peaceful, fast asleep. I sat in the rocker next to her watching her. I watched her and cried, cried for the child that I brought into this world and plagued with this ordeal. I thought about the obstacles that lay ahead for her. This poor, innocent child, only on this earth for three years and burdened with such problems. I remember as a child always hearing the grownups say, "as long as you have your health, you have everything." At thirty-five years of age, I finally, truly, and deeply understood the meaning of it. Would Rayna have "everything?" Would she have her health?

"Can I get you anything?"

I looked up to see a compassionate nurse smiling at me. I knew she probably meant something to eat or drink, but all I could think of for an answer was to give my baby back to me, whole, unharmed, and unaffected by this ordeal. I just wanted to turn back the clock, return to a time when none of this had happened, when I worried about which day would be better to have the car serviced, which store had the better buy on winter jackets, and not which doctor, which hospital, which procedure would give us the only answer we wanted to hear.

I shook my head no to the nurse and flashed her a one hundred percent fake smile with complete conviction that she knew was one hundred percent just that.

Rayna woke up, looked at me, confused, then smiled. I smiled at her. I took her hand. Her small hand just folded inside mine; that is, her left hand. It was the only one she could fold in mine.

"Hi, honey, I love you." Her response came in another big, Rayna smile.

I looked up at the nurse with tears in my eyes. She handed me a Kleenex and gave me a tender pat on the back. I admired the nursing profession.

It was time to transfer Rayna to her temporary home for the night. As we passed the waiting room on the way to her room, I stopped to pick up my jacket, but found only empty chairs and scattered magazines. My jacket was missing. I inquired all over the hospital, soon to realize that my jacket most likely had been stolen. I was enraged, not because a fifty dollar parka had been taken, but because at this moment, I had already been slapped in the face by life, how could anyone do this to me at such a vulnerable time? Why would anyone do something so callous and invasive as taking my property? I felt stripped, stripped of my harmonious life, my perfect family.

I was enraged, not because of the monetary value of the jacket (which the hospital insisted on reimbursing, and I in turn gave the money back as a donation), not for the fashion of the jacket, but for the challenge, when what I really needed was the support. The rational side of me was enraged at the evil act of stealing. My sympathetic side quietly forgave the culprit for stealing. It was the week before Christmas. Perhaps this was a homeless person, a poor person in need of warmth for his child. My heart forgave him, my head never could. Stealing is stealing and it is wrong. After all, even Jean Valjean went to jail.

As night approached, Rayna and I snuggled together in the bed. Allyn went home to be with Tovah. Rayna's eating pattern was off, and at three o'clock she woke up starving. The nurse brought her some juice, crackers, and peanut butter. We sat together in bed, in the quiet of the night, as Rayna filled her stomach. Occasionally, we'd hear a baby cry, followed by the footsteps of a nurse echoing down the corridor. We called it a picnic. To this day, Rayna remembers that picnic in the middle of the night and exactly what she had to eat. She speaks about it like another child might fondly remember a day at an amusement park. I'm glad her memories of that night are positive. Let me be the one to remember the anxieties.

We did have a roommate, a small child who just stared, no expression, no laughter, no tears, no life to her other than bodily functions. My heart went out to the mother. I noticed the mother was pregnant. I admired her, bringing another child into the world when she was plagued with a sick one. I don't know if I could be that brave. If Rayna had been my firstborn, I don't know if I would have the courage to bring another child into this world. Thank goodness she wasn't. Thank God I had my beautiful Tovah, and with some prayers, I would have Rayna "returned" to me. Yes, I admired that mother.

In the morning, I awoke first. I was captivated by Rayna's sleeping innocence and her peaceful face. Would she awake frightened, disoriented, timid of her new surroundings? All cuddled under the soft blanket, a temporary escape from reality, I wanted to freeze the moment. I didn't want to go back in time to the horrors that brought us to this moment; yet I didn't want to go forward to the impending news of Rayna's test results.

The other child was not in the room, and the mother was watching a news show on the single television that serviced the whole room. She had the sound turned down. Shortly, Rayna awoke and asked to watch *Sesame Street.* I called out to the mother asking her to please change the station for my daughter. The mother was totally annoyed with me, and as she reluctantly changed the channel, she indignantly informed me, that *she* was watching a show. Did I miss something here? Aren't we in a children's hospital? Aren't the children the patients, not us? Aren't they the sick ones? I lost my admiration for her. I wanted to be understanding of her agony from an experienced vantage point. I retained my sympathy for her problems, but my admiration disappeared.

Shortly after breakfast, as we were packing our things to return home, the doctor entered, followed by Allyn. Allyn brought me another jacket; the doctor brought us the results. The arteriogram was negative, no vascular problem; the tumor was confirmed. I put on my jacket and stood shivering with the chills.

Chapter Three

HALF BOTTLE OF CHAMPAGNE

Okay, so, now we're back to the final diagnosis. If it isn't a bleeding problem, then the mass is being caused by a tumor, and the only way to determine exactly what kind of tumor it was, was to perform a stereotactic biopsy. It was considered intense surgery; a needle would have to travel down into the area, extract some of the mass, and be sent off to pathology for determination. There were approximately six kinds of tumors that this could be. One could be benign and the other five, various degrees of malignancies. Because of the intricacies of this operation, the finite, precise details of getting the needle into the exact location of the mass, much preparation had to be done, and the biopsy was scheduled for exactly six weeks. Six weeks for a team of doctors to prepare for the operation, and six weeks for me to prepare my mind, my life, and to try to keep some normalcy in the family. Defining the new meaning of normalcy was going to be an interesting assignment for me.

That definition included my approach to how to continue disciplining her. How do you tell a child to pick up her toys and put them away because that is the rule, so that she will know where they are the next time, when you don't know the future? Will there be a next time? And rules? The rules of life? The ones that guarantee us health and happiness? Or was it just an unrealistic fantasy of mine that I would bring a child into this world and she would have health? No guarantees there. As hard as I tried to continue with any semblance of decorum and discipline, I fell short, very short.

If Rayna had said, "Jump, Mommy," the only logical answer I could possibly have thought of at that time would be, "How high?"

"I want some bread, Mommy."

"Really, Rayna? What kind, honey? White, whole wheat, rye? Or would you like that wonderful sourdough from San Francisco? What time is the next plane? I'll get right on, fly to San Francisco, pick up a loaf or two, or twenty, and be right back." Oh, Rayna, why did this have to happen to you?

Small tasks became big tasks, big tasks became monumental tasks and monumental tasks became impossible. And if I thought the big G (guilt) took over my life, it soon had competition from the big P (that's right, paranoia). I found myself at a complete loss over how to deal with Rayna, how to say no, how not to be at her beck and call, not that she asked me to be, but that was how I perceived it, or how I wanted it to be. I knew in reality we all needed order to our lives, but then I'd flip the coin and the other side told me to get an extra loaf of that sourdough bread. I would start to panic if I didn't say yes to every request. I would have trouble saying she couldn't stay up and watch that extra show, in the desperate hope to keep a schedule, or saying no to that extra toy at the toy store because I had just bought her a trillion at the last one. I had unreasonable feelings that whichever request I said no to, if she didn't survive this ordeal (my euphemism for die—unthinkable word in my vocabulary), I'd remember the night I told her she couldn't watch that show. I would panic that every decision was wrong and everything would come back to haunt me. In fact, I was beating myself up. I needed to set limits, boundaries—her boundaries, my boundaries—find a happy medium to all this.

But alas, it's amazing how your stamina grows. My stress grew, but so did my endurance. I thought I could handle anything now, until Allyn came home with a paper.

"If anything went wrong during surgery..."It was a letter he had drafted at work that day, requesting that they not resuscitate her for any reason, should her heart stop beating. Sign this? I've signed many things in my life, bank checks, a marriage certificate, permission slips for school trips, not a permission slip to stop my daughter's life. I looked at the paper. "In the event of..." I looked at Allyn, standing there with pen in hand. So cut-and-dry, so scientific, so matter-of-fact, but I knew deep down he was hurting as badly as I was. He raised his eyes for my answer. Allyn felt strongly that this should be signed by the two of us before presenting it to the doctors. It should be a mutual decision. Two-parent, mutual decisions—four words, four simple words, not always.

Since having Tovah and Rayna, we have had our disagreements on how to raise them. I always knew we wouldn't agree on everything. We came from different backgrounds, were raised differently, and we had to find our own set of criteria for bringing up our children. I guess it's like the perfect recipe, a few ingredients from his upbringing, a few from mine, and a unique blend of Sandy and Allyn.

I thought about a time when we stood in a store absolutely at opposite ends of a decision. Although, not a deep-rooted decision, it did bring to the surface some of our philosophical differences in child rearing.

Tovah was, and still is to this day, not a status-symbol seeker. She buys a pair of shorts or shirt based on its comfort, looks, and necessity—not whether it has an alligator or some other symbol on it. I'm proud of her for her placement of values.

The Champion brand of sweatshirts had just emerged on the market, and its influx was overwhelming—like the Beatles on the Ed Sullivan show. One day Tovah mentioned she "might like one of those sweatshirts, they're nice." Not a demand for one, not a status-seeking comment like "I must own one of those," just a casual desire to have one.

Standing in a department store one day, Allyn and I chose a pretty color sweatshirt to surprise Tovah. He then insisted on buying one for Rayna. I informed him that Rayna had no interest in this kind of sweatshirt. Knowing the intense popularity of these sweatshirts, he was adamant in his decision.

"I'm not buying Tovah a Champion without buying Rayna one and that's that."

My attempts to explain that Rayna had no interest in this type of clothing fell on deaf ears.

"If you want to buy Rayna a surprise, make it something she wants; a doll, or a pretend cooking set, not a plain sweatshirt with some writing on it announcing the name of a company. She has no interest in these."

My pleas went unanswered. We left the store with two Champion sweatshirts, one satisfied Allyn, and one frustrated Sandy.

Upon opening their unexpected gifts, Tovah's eyes bugged out with sheer joy, while Rayna's fell in disappointment. And, being the wonderful, appreciative, unspoiled children they are, Tovah hugged us with genuine thanks and Rayna hugged us with camouflaged disappointment. Later that night, Tovah was wondering if Rayna might like to trade colors.

"Rayna, Tovah asked me if you would like to trade colors on your Champions."

Rayna looked at me very seriously, and replied, "What's a Champion?"

I was going to have to work on the compromise division of our marriage.

There were other decisions not always agreed upon:

bedtime hours, appropriate age for walking alone from school or to the playground, how much television; and there would be future decisions of when to be home on a date, when to wear makeup, which was the best college. Decisions about life. But, always, it was how to live it, not *whether* to live it. How does one sign this piece of paper?

The sweatshirt incident seemed so silly. Opposite sides of the fence, different ideals, values, hopes, dreams. Allyn handed me the pen. I signed my name—just above his.

The following week was the beginning of the holiday season, and we had planned a trip to Florida months ago. Although we were starting to get different opinions on how to treat Rayna, one thing on which everyone did agree was that this condition would not change in one week, how to treat it would not be determined in one week, and there was no need to cancel a week of fun in the sun. Surrendering to their expert opinions, we packed bathing suits and light clothes and were on our way. The only thing heavy we took with us were our hearts. We decided the doctors were right; a week wouldn't make a difference. We might as well be miserable in eighty degree weather instead of twenty. The sunshine would not make our problems go away, just camouflage them for seven days. We would be staying with wonderful cousins whom I adored, who doted on us with nurturing love. That was just the prescription we all needed. Doting and nurturing, taken as needed, with unlimited refills.

This was also the time when Cabbage Patch dolls were the hottest item, when you waited in line for them at the toy store, taking a number in hopes they wouldn't sell out before you had a chance to be the proud owner of Jennifer Felicia or Mary Bethany. Each of the girls had been given her own Cabbage Patch doll months before, both thrilled in possessing one, treasuring the dolls and spoiling them with all the love children give to pretend beings.

We talked about buying them second ones. I had mixed feelings. I wanted them to appreciate the ones they had and I didn't want to spoil them. Of course, all it would take is one little request from a certain three-year-old whose health was in a precarious state, and I'd be on the next plane to the Cabbage Patch factory itself. I was trying to think straight, a difficult task at the least. For the moment, they each had one Cabbage Patch doll and cherished it.

Sitting by the pool, I watched other children splashing about, diving in, swimming around with both hands moving, screaming with joy and carefree happiness, as children should be.

"Look, Grandma, watch me dive."

"Look, Dad, look what I can do." And the boy would do a handstand in the pool.

We sat by the pool desperately trying to have fun in the sun as the doctors had ordered. Rayna sat on the edge of the pool, timid, afraid. I walked over to her, sat next to her. Her bright pink suit proudly displayed a sparkling butterfly, her left shoulder a gob of sunscreen that I didn't rub in enough. I put my arm around her, made the lotion disappear into her skin, cushioned her head on my shoulder, and whispered, "I need a friend to go in the water with me."

Rayna grabbed my hand and we slowly walked into the pool together. When we felt that first sensation of cool, refreshing water wash over our bodies, Rayna giggled. What a melodious sound. Maybe she wasn't screaming, or shouting to have her dive watched, but she giggled, and she was happy. Her left hand clung to my neck as I took her for a swim. For a brief moment, all the worries of real life could disappear in the swirl of the water, in the tropical paradise of a luxurious week. My moment of bliss, of shutting off the rest of the world was broken by Allyn's words to come see him.

Allyn was reading a Fort Lauderdale paper and he had noticed an advertisement for a place selling Cabbage Patch dolls and thought we should surprise the girls. I panicked. I thought I was going to try to show restraint, not spoil them, but somehow my heart lost out to my head and within minutes we dried off from our swim, got dressed and drove forty-five minutes to some special store. Several dollars later, Jennifer

Felicia and Mary Bethany had playmates, and our Cabbage Patch doll inventory doubled. So much for trying to keep a sense of order. I guess when you've been told your three-year-old has a brain tumor, most likely malignant, a forty-five minute drive in a car on a beautiful beach day in an unfamiliar state, to a toy store doesn't seem out of line. We needed help.

And so we got help. The plane had barely touched down at Logan Airport, the cab had scarcely delivered us safely home, and our shorts were hardly replaced by winter coats, before we were on the phone, networking to find the perfect child psychologist. One of our easier and wiser decisions. A wonderfully warm and compassionate woman, she helped us sort all of this out, put everything in its proper place, almost like unpacking in a new house. We had been thrown into this unfamiliar situation. Why did we think we could familiarize ourselves with it alone? As we had gone to neurologists to help us with the medical part of the problem, it seemed only logical to go to a psychologist to help us with the emotional part of it.

Through the years we have consulted a variety of psychologists and they have all been a source of strength and encouragement to help keep us straight on a crooked path.

Rayna and Tovah spent the rest of these six weeks doing what they had basically been doing all along—going to school, playing with friends, and just being kids. Allyn went to work, and in his free time took up temporary residency at a table at Harvard University's Countway Medical Library, trying to absorb everything there was to learn about tumors. This was his way of fighting back, of endeavoring to deal with this uncontrollable disease. He read, underlined, xeroxed, and came home with piles of journals, colorfully decorated in yellow highlight: "Cases of this nature are limited...," "...No defined, successful treatment to date..."

And me? I tried to do it all: be the glue to keep the family together, the gasoline to keep the family going, the comic to keep the family laughing, the mother, the wife, the cook, the chauffeur, the peacemaker, and the strong one. Smiles for the public; tears for the private.

"Oh, we're hanging in there. Thanks for asking."

"Thanks for calling, I'll let you know if there's anything..."

And for those who were acquaintances, not local people, the rare people you see once in a while, an old history teacher, a former neighbor from your old apartment building, the ones who screamed, "Hey, Sandy, how you doing? Long time, no see. How are the girls?"

Tovah is in kindergarten mastering blocks and coloring, and Rayna has a brain tumor.

"Fine, thanks for asking."

Mostly my free time was spent exercising. I would walk around a track, thinking, and then willing myself not to think, but I always lost. Every step, every thought was about Rayna. And every other step and every other thought was about Tovah. Poor child, how can she even begin to comprehend all this. The most I went through as a child was an older brother with a bicycle accident. It was scary, but he was okay, or my other brother suddenly rushed to the hospital with an appendectomy, also scary, but done and over with, both brothers fully recovered. This upset to the family was so uncertain, and I didn't know just how long the road was going to be.

I would walk around the track, earphones in place, listening to songs written for lovers, intended for romantic situations; boy meets girl, girl falls in love with boy, boy and girl live happily ever after, but the only words I heard were for Rayna. Every song, once having those original, intended meanings for me, now took on different meanings. Words meant for lovers, to me, meant words for a mother and daughter.

"I'll Never Leave You" didn't mean two lovers never breaking up, but a daughter reassuring a mother she'll be all right or a mother reassuring a daughter she'll always be by her side.

"My Girl" wasn't some boy's girlfriend, but my Rayna. "I've Got You and You've Got Me," why Rayna and me, or Tovah and me, of course. Was there any other interpretation?

Some days, I would walk with a friend, and then the music would be abandoned for talk. I would verbalize my feelings, my fears. One day I would be totally convinced that the biopsy would be my friend and show kindness, be forgiving, spare Rayna, and the next moment I saw it as the enemy. Then I would dig my sneakers harder into the track, walk a little faster, talk a little faster—like that would make it go away.

And because it is really true that you can't make time stand still, all of a sudden the biopsy was only two days away, but a curve ball was thrown into the field and changed the course of things. Just prior to Rayna's admission, the suggestion to try a new, experimental procedure was made by Allyn. He had just heard of the NMR, the nuclear magnetic resonance.

The doctors did not really see the point in this, since they already had a CAT scan, and the arteriogram had proven that it wasn't a blood vessel problem, there really would be nothing to gain from performing this test. The arteriogram had shown the lesion was not vascular and the CAT scan already proved a mass existed. Therefore, the NMR wouldn't be of any benefit. Had the arteriogram come back positive, then the need for an NMR would be warranted. But because Allyn never leaves a stone unturned, the doctors turned this one. It was so experimental at this time, that we had to "sign our lives away" with liability and insurance, but...all of Allyn's stones must be turned.

It was a bitter cold January day. I bundled up Rayna, lingering just a bit longer than necessary, as I tightened her collar, protecting her from the cold. The least I could do for her is protect her from the elements, keep her as warm as possible. Rayna sat in front. She looked so cute, snow jacket, fuzzy winter hat with the pom-pom on top with the frayed yarn at the end. She listened to one of her tapes. As Old McDonald declared sounds about his farm, I drove. As Rayna belted out her rendition, screaming, "ee, i, ee i, o," I approached the hospital and had to tell her it was time to transform from a three-year-old singing star to a victim of unfortunate medical circumstances.

"We're here, honey," is how I summarized it.

I pulled up to the front of the hospital, dropping Allyn and Rayna off, then parked the car. Allyn must have repeated three times where to meet him, and I readily assured him I heard him and knew where to go. I dropped them off, watched the two of them escape into the warmth of the building, then proceeded to park my car. These garages where you go around and around and around were beginning to annoy me. Funny, I had never been irritated by them before.

I walked through the bitter wind into the hospital and stopped short. I didn't have the foggiest idea where to go. Spotting two doctors walking down the corridor, I stopped them, and asked where I could find the NMR.

"You want an enema?" (No, but instead I'll take a healthy daughter.)

When I started to repeat NMR, I realized I was about to do something I hadn't done in almost two months, laugh. It did help, it did make me feel better for at least a minute or two. I walked into the NMR (now also called MRI, magnetic resonance imaging, as common today as the VCR), as Allyn was unloading every piece of metal he had, car keys, coins, watches, etc. for the machine is exactly what it says, magnetic. One of the positive features of this machine is that there is no radiation emitted to the patient.

I repeated my story to Allyn.

"He thought I said 'En-e-ma.' Get it?"

He laughed. I laughed. I tried to explain it to Rayna.

"See, honey, The initials NMR can sound like en-e-ma and an enema is when…"

Always the teacher, always the giver of information, helping her grow, helping her take her place in the world, always using any opportunity to give her a life experience. We all laughed. Yes, life was going to be good for us. All we needed were a few prayers, lots of luck, and some miracles. Not too much to ask.

As was becoming a common practice, I sat in the waiting room waiting for the test to be over. Rayna seemed to have her preferences: Mommy to cuddle with, her favorite lap to sit on, read a story to her, but Daddy was the one to stay with her for the tests, to be by her side as the IV was administered, as she was wheeled under the complex machinery of an MRI or CAT scan. So, I became a "waiting room expert." I could now flip through a magazine in record speed and copy a recipe using great abbreviations.

"Heat ov—350—blend above ing—let cl—frz wl." When I planned to cook all these gourmet, low fat, cholesterol, man-pleasing, in-less-than-five-minute meals was a mystery, and in reality, of no consequence. I was the waiting room queen and I could do anything I wanted. Did you know that the carpet in the second room over on the sixth floor has three hundred squigglies in its design?

My pocketbook became the family's minisuitcase for appointment cards, Rayna's winter hat, a favorite book, crayons, extra paper, papers with information about "your child's procedure," and the most delicious never-to-be-made recipes from every magazine possible. I hate to cook.

When the test was over, Rayna emerged from the room with Allyn. I had just finished writing "Srvs 16," threw my pencil into my little "suitcase," and hugged Rayna. Another day, another test. When will it end? Her main and only concern—lunch—Chinese chicken wings from a Chinese restaurant at Faneuil Hall Market. (Good thing it wasn't sourdough bread—we had to be back at the hospital in a few hours to be admitted—making it a little tough to get to San Francisco and back.)

As we exited the hospital, back into the harsh wind and bitter temperatures, Allyn leaned over and whispered some of the most beautiful words he ever said to me since, "I do."

"Sandy, don't get your hopes up, but the NMR shows there's a chance that this isn't a solid tumor after all. There was hemorrhaging and the rest of the mass is blood vessels."

I gasped, then broke into a hop, skip, and jump, looking around for those two doctors. I wanted to tell them that was the best "enema!!"

Sitting among the real world of people having lunch, I watched as Rayna ate her chicken wings with relish. I sat with my hands cupped about a coffee cup vicariously enjoying her lunch. Children are wonderful. The NMR experience, still so fresh in my mind, was probably long-forgotten in hers. The present, the yummy chicken wings, the colorful surroundings, the bustling crowd of diverse people grabbing lunch—that was all that she saw. The NMR was history to her.

The next day, we still checked into the hospital, for it was yet to be determined if these results were definite. Pre-op tests were done, as usual, with a repeat NMR. The next morning, Rayna was still not allowed to eat anything until a definite decision was made. To keep her mind off food we wheeled her around in a "go-kart," sort of an elongated stroller/wheelchair combination. After seeing all the interesting sights of the hospital, we were paged to go back to the room, the doctor would be there in a few minutes to discuss the final outcome of this. Tumor or no tumor? Biopsy or no biopsy? Bottle of champagne or a box of Kleenex? Rayna and I snuggled back on the hospital bed as Allyn went to answer a page on his beeper.

A woman entered the room with a walk of fear, with doom on her face as she approached the balding child in the bed across from us. Another woman followed cautiously behind her, lingering closer to the door. I heard the little girl, say, "Hi, Mommy" and knew why the look of doom had covered the woman's face. I had also overheard the doctor say something about terminal.

"Aunt Betty is here to see you," I heard the mother say. The child mustered a weak smile. But Aunt Betty was really visiting the door of the room. She hung back, forcing happy smiles on her so very sick niece. I had once heard that people visiting dying people in the hospital sometimes have a hard time entering the room. They would cling to the doorway, afraid to approach the terminal patient. It seemed that the sicker the person, the closer to the door the visitor would cling. I hoped this child wasn't dying, that all the medical treatments in the world would give her more than only the six years of life she had.

I tried not to look at the pain on the mother's face, the lack of life on the child's face, and the look of fear and wonderment on Aunt Betty's. I felt sympathy for her. For the moment, I felt safe. I didn't get news from a doctor like this mother might have received.

"I'm sorry, Mrs...but your child has...We'll do the best we can, but..."

I wouldn't allow myself to think about getting news like that. My concentration had to be on the positive, the present. "No news was good news" was going to be my slogan of the day.

A nurse entered the room with a determined stride and a definite look on her face. She stared right at me, announcing that the doctor would be there in a few minutes to discharge Rayna, to pack our bags and get ready to leave. The NMR showed that Rayna's lesion was caused by malformed blood vessels that bled and left a huge mass; no cancer and no operation. Our nightmare was now only a bad dream. Champagne, not Kleenex, was the order of the day. But, I chose the box of Kleenex, the whole box, because I couldn't stop the happy tears. They just kept coming.

The enemy hadn't disappeared, just retreated for the time being. Rayna still had serious problems, and although I couldn't open a whole bottle of champagne, I could open half of it. Someday, we would open a whole bottle, someday. I believed that. I had to believe that. I wouldn't allow any other choice.

True to form, we did what the doctor said. We packed our bags and went home. No biopsy, no ten-inch needle being sunk into my daughter's brain, no shaving of her head, no paper needed on that day with hesitant signatures giving permission to stop resuscitation, or that she could bleed and become a "vegetable."

Entering the house, everything looked wonderful. The couch looked so inviting, comfortable, safe. The kitchen seemed brighter, the floor shinier. And that annoying stain on the hardwood floors seemed so insignificant. How could I have ever been annoyed by that stain in the past?

And the best part of coming home that day—I went up to the school, stood outside Tovah's kindergarten room, and relished the look of utter surprise when she walked out of class and found me there instead of the designated caretaker for the day. She dropped her artful masterpiece of a tree with a little girl under it and a rainbow above it and threw her little arms around me, yelling, "Mommy." She felt delicious, smelled delicious. I explained that her sister didn't need the operation and we could all go home together. Tucking her hand in mine, we left school to go home and get ready for dinner, dinner for four...takeout.

Life looked pretty good right now—challenging—but good. I guess everything is relative after all. I was so appreciative of the fact that Rayna didn't have a malignant brain tumor, that I actually got on the coffee table in my living room and did a victory dance. For the moment I was happy. For the moment life didn't look so bleak.

I thought about that feeling. How everything does have its counterpart to put things into perspective. But why must it be that way? Why can't we appreciate what we have without seeing the other side of it? Do we have to have ten straight days of rain before we can appreciate a sunny day? Do we have to sleep on a lumpy mattress while visiting someone before we appreciate the comfort of our own bed? Why do we have to experience the negative before we can appreciate the positive?

The reason the arteriogram was negative was because Rayna's mass was caused by a venous malformation which characteristically does not show up on the arterial study. Modern technological advances in medicine and Allyn's persistence had saved my child. The timing was uncanny. If this bleed had happened only a year earlier, without the availability of the MRI, the biopsy would have been the only alternative.

The answers weren't good, yet not as bad. But, for now, all I got was half of a bottle of champagne.

Chapter Four

AND LIFE GOES ON

Up until now, the one thing that every doctor with whom we consulted, and there were many, throughout the world, had agreed upon, was to do a stereotactic biopsy to determine what kind of tumor it was. Now that it was determined not to be a tumor, we needed to know what to do next. Here is where the roads divided, and we had to decide which path to follow, which one would lead us to the pot of gold.

Remember, the enemy had only retreated, not held up the white flag. We found this to be more difficult than we had anticipated. For almost as many doctors as we consulted, there were equally as many opinions. I remembered the joke that a second opinion is fine as long as it agrees with the first. We got a varied selection of roads to take. What Rayna had was called a cavernous hemangioma, a collection of malformed blood vessels that bled. This is not common. Where it occurred in the brain was in the left thalamus. This made her condition even more rare. Therefore the solution of how to deal with it was not a simple one.

As our phone bills rose due to seeking advice from doctors throughout the world, so did our frustrations upon hearing their conflicting opinions. No one had any good information about the natural history of a lesion of this nature. It was rare, very rare. And because it was such a rare lesion, a unique condition, information was sparse. Textbooks, journals, neuroanatomists, neurophysiologists, neuropathologists, and neurologists were among the many sources on Allyn's checklist. There wasn't even a series of ten people with this disorder to give us any reliable or valid statistics. We were floating in a big sea with a very small paddle.

Over the past few weeks, little scraps of paper started piling up on Allyn's desk. He would have information written down from every doctor's visit, every telephone call, everyone he talked to. He found himself with a huge pile of notes written on everything from a scrap of paper to the parking garage ticket stub to a napkin. One night he sat and systematically recorded all the pertinent information into an organized notebook filled with doctor's names, names of clinics, even the secretaries' names. It was Rayna's directory, a map to find the cure. The next thing Allyn did was make a back-up copy to keep at home, in fear of losing this "bible."

Several doctors felt we ought to go ahead and radiate it. While this would definitely cauterize the area and prevent any further bleeding, negative side effects could include damage to other parts of the brain or a malignancy in an area where no malignancy presently existed. Others felt operating would be a better way to go. Although there were major risks factors from paralysis to mortality, this would definitely remove the malformation, which in their opinion outweighed the risks. Then there were others who felt that there was a strong possibility that this was a one-time bleed and the possibility existed that it may never bleed again.

There were definitely strong opponents to operating because of its inaccessibility. Due to the nature of this malformation, the actual bleeding-out process is not life-threatening as it occurs, but could eventually be, as well as the further damage it would leave in its wake. In other words, if she were to have another bleed, we would have to make a decision about intervention, i.e. surgery or radiation, but for right now, this group of doctors felt the best treatment for Rayna, was no treatment. I called these people the Leave Alone Group. They strongly believed in following the Hippocratic Oath, "*Primum Non Nocere*." "First do no harm " meant no invasive therapy because of its great unknown status.

How utterly frustrating to have such varying opinions. Rayna's case was indeed complex, as were the answers, if there were any answers. Operate? Radiate? Leave alone? No perfect answer, but did I really expect a perfect answer, a miracle? Yes.

It was like a horse race.

"And Radiation is off, wait, I see Surgery inching up to Radiation. Yes, ladies and gentlemen, it's going to be a close race, for Leave Alone has just given Radiation and Surgery some fierce competition. Who will win this race today, this race for life, this race for health? Looks pretty close, tough to tell who's in the lead. Wait, look at that, can you believe it? Leave Alone just took a major leap and looks like it's going to take the lead. But, here come Radiation and Surgery. Looks like a three way tie, but Leave Alone has inched forward and wins this race by a narrow margin. Whew, this is one announcer who is exhausted from such a close, tense race. Congratulations to all the participants and good luck in future races."

I need to stop daydreaming. It really impedes facing reality. No, change that. I need to continue daydreaming. It helps face reality.

That is so true. We are born into this world through no voluntary decision of our own. And from the moment we do enter this world, we are victims of circumstance, victims of uncontrollable external influences on our life. We have no control over things like the weather. Nor are we in the driver's seat when it comes to illness and to sadness. These are dropped in our lap whether we want them or not. To obtain happiness in life, we must seek it. Happiness is not something that automatically comes our way; it takes more active participation; whereas illness can be delivered without us consciously seeking it. We can be passive recipients, passive victims.

And so, we finally decided to "go with" the group of doctors who expressed the *laissez-faire* approach, the Leave Alones, and watch its course. We wouldn't be taking all the serious risks of surgery, nor would we be exposing her to negative side effects of radiation. We would merely be sitting with a time bomb in her head that may or may not go off at some future date.

We selected Dr. Robert DeLong to be Rayna's neurologist at the Massachusetts General Hospital. So, now all we had to do was leave it alone. Simple. Watch it. Simple. Pray that it never bled again. Simple. Have those prayers answered. Not so simple.

Unless something changed in Rayna's medical status, we would see Dr. DeLong twice a year for clinical checkups and once a year for an MRI. This went along fine for three years until something did change, not in Rayna's status, but in Dr. DeLong's. He announced to us that he would be leaving the Boston area and moving to North Carolina to be at Duke University Hospital, the head of Pediatric Neurology. We were very sorry to see this happen. Rayna had "grown up" with this doctor with her illness and we were not about to let him go. He represented so much to us. He was a doctor, a source of strength that gave hope to Rayna, as well as a nurturing, kind individual.

This decision had a bigger impact on me than I allowed myself to feel. It pointed out how very vulnerable we were in this situation. This wasn't an injury that we could put a Band-Aid on, or dispense Tylenol. We were so dependent on outside sources for help, so vulnerable to so many people who were taking part in Rayna's cure. Therefore, instead, of just letting this wonderful source slip through our hands and out of our lives, out of Rayna's life, we opted for the next best thing to having Dr. DeLong in Boston. Every September we fly to Duke University to have the continued care from Dr. DeLong, and in the six months in between, we see another wonderful neurologist in Boston, Dr. Elizabeth Dooling.

Who said you can't have the best of both worlds?

I think one of the most challenging aspects of Rayna's illness was that sea of unknown. Although no one holds the future in his hands, there are some things more predictable than others. I tried to get used to the fact that each and every day of her life was like walking on eggshells, that her condition was unstable and at any point the blood vessels, now at rest, could betray Rayna and bleed. That was the long term challenge; the everyday, short-term challenge was something else.

One of the more difficult times was when Rayna suddenly "woke up" and became aware; when she was no longer oblivious to the fact that she was the only one who couldn't tie her shoes, or that the other children could run faster than she. This awareness of her own fragility was one of the more painful times of facing the ugly truth about what this bleed had done to my daughter. Her symptoms are very similar to that of a stroke victim with weakened muscles. In Rayna's case, she is weakened from head to toe on the right side.

And once she "woke up," the questions came like a gusher:

"How come everyone can tie their shoes and I can't?"

"Why can't I run as fast as everyone in my class?"

Yes, awareness had definitely set in. Rayna was no longer insulated, unaware of her differences. Her hand was weakened, her leg was weakened, but her eyes were now wide open and her mind very alert. She saw and felt things that I only wish I could protect her from, yet knew that was an impossibility.

And if you think the "why can't I" questions were painful, it was the "will I ever be able to" questions that sent me reeling, my heart pounding and breaking.

"Will I ever be able to drive a car?"

"Will I ever be able to use my right hand?"

"Will I ever be able to walk without a limp?"

"Will I ever have babies?"

These were the times I resented the most, when I felt the most vulnerable, the most angry, the most victimized.

As strong as I tried to be, I would falter, and when Rayna cried, I would cry along beside her. But, these turned out to be moments of bonding. I'd hold her in my arms, feel her try desperately to hug me, but all that she could do was get one hand around me. Rayna has so much love to give, and she couldn't even hug me with two hands. Her heart wants to, her right hand wouldn't let her. So, I would get the most wonderful one-handed hugs in the world. She'd put her head on my shoulder and I'd stroke her hair and always say one important thing to her—something positive, no matter what the situation. We would never end our little talks together without a positive, hopeful word, a word of encouragement. Every tearful outburst and every talk always ended the same way, with a positive word from me and a beautiful smile from Rayna.

One of the tactics I always endeavored to take in discussing Rayna's frustrations was the optimistic approach. When Rayna would lament about something she was not able to do, I would retort with a comment, like a bolt of lightning, about all the things that she can do. I would always acknowledge her concerns, never dismiss them. I would listen to her frustrations, acknowledge her feelings, then move on. I think a big secret to handling a lot of problems is learning how to move on—sometimes easier said than done.

"I'm terrible at bouncing a ball."

"And you're wonderful at tennis," I would readily reply.

"No good at soccer."

"Fabulous at singing."

"Can't even tie my shoe."

"Mastered putting the toothpaste on."

"Can't do this."

"Can do this."

"Can't do…"

"Can do…"

"Bad at…"

"Wonderful at…"

I would go tit for tat with her until she finally saw what I was getting at, or until I got a big smile. They were both positive messages to me.

"Rayna, I know it hurts, I know it's frustrating, but I also know you are strong and doing the best you can. I am so proud of you. I always have and I always will be."

Sometimes, Tovah would walk by Rayna's room, ask what was going on, and of course, we now became a trio, a harmonious trio.

"We're just having a moment."

Tovah would see my tear-stained face, approach me, put her arms around me. We were a chain, a welded chain, each seeking strength from the other, each giving our best, a ladies' club, bonded and united. I share many of my frustrations about Rayna with Tovah. After all, she is my friend, partner, someone I share my life with.

As Rayna got older, the gap got wider. As children were developing more motor skills, Rayna was still struggling with the ones that were impaired. The gap got wider, Rayna became more aware, and the visits to the child psychologist increased.

I kept believing in the premise that time and aging would erase some of the frailties that plagued Rayna. I refused to admit that she might never tie her shoe; but instead, told myself that she would just be a little delayed in accomplishing this task. This had to be my optimistic tendencies emerging, my insulation against believing that she would never manage these small tasks, or at least not within the "normal allotment" for mastering a task.

"Soon, Rayna, we'll keep working on that shoe and someday we'll get it tied."

I didn't know when someday was. I didn't know if she

would conquer that task today, tomorrow, or some obscure date in the future. What I did know is that she never gave up, and she had a future.

The occupational therapist worked on it, I worked on it, and Rayna worked on her shoe—a team of three dedicated people. I have never given up believing that Rayna will tie her shoe. I only now accept the fact that her accomplishments are not age-related. The day I give up believing that Rayna will tie her shoe is the day I give up believing—period.

So life settled into the new life that we now had. My vocabulary expanded with words like occupational therapy, physical therapy, cavernous hemangioma, right hemiparesis. One of the first requests made of us as life tried to get back to normal came from the psychologist. She said she very rarely gave a patient a direct order, but she was making an exception for Allyn and myself. For three months, we had done nothing but focus our lives on our children and now that life was back to "normal," it would be "advisable and in the best interest of our marriage as well as for the children's sake" that we went out socially. She felt that not only would this do us a world of good, it would show the children that things were okay.

"I really think it's time the two of you spend some time alone."

"The last time I spent any time alone with my husband, Doctor, I returned to an environment not to my liking."

"You can't dwell on the past."

"And I can't accept the present."

So, with much reluctance, but acknowledging the logic of what the doctor suggested, we planned a night out. As it turned out, there was a charity dinner coming up and we knew quite a few people going, so we decided this would be our first venture out. We paid our money and wrote down on the form the people we would like to be seated with, as the form requested. When that night came, I looked at Rayna and Tovah and knew there was no way I was going out. Forget what the doctor said, forget her expert recommendation. I announced this decision to Allyn, and he said he understood and half an hour later we were dressed and out the door. I guess I didn't do a great job convincing him—or me!

We entered the hall, picked up our place card, and attempted to socialize. I noticed eyes turning our way, looks of sympathy, looks of puzzlement, concern, anguish, curiosity, friendly smiles, warm smiles. I felt like the actor, everyone in expectation of my lines, my delivery, the latest bulletin on Rayna's progress. I didn't know exactly who knew about Rayna and who didn't, but I could almost tell by the eyes.

I had an overwhelming feeling of abandonment, despite the fact that both girls were home baking brownies with a baby sitter, reading books, and probably the last thing they were thinking about was us! When it came time to sit down, we realized that none of the people at our table were the ones we had requested on the registration form. I approached the person in charge of reservations, only to find quite a few people ahead of me. Evidently something had gone wrong. The man in charge was trying to explain that he was sorry and that he would try to fix it. When it came time for me, I must have been the "straw that broke the camel's back," because he turned to me with just a little bit more annoyance than I could handle.

"Okay, so something went wrong. Can't you just sit with someone else, make a new friend or something. After all, if you get this upset over something as minor as this, what are you going to do when you have real problems in life?"

And that was my first venture back to the social world.

And life goes on.

(And the man taking the reservations has now become a good friend of ours.) So, for the "Reservationist," life goes on.

Living with Rayna's illness brought daily awakenings for me, as well. On any given day, a thought could pop into my head that I had never dreamed of happening. In the myriad of doctor's appointments, sitting on one leather couch after another, rotely repeating Rayna's story, one basic question was universally asked.

"Any questions? Anything I didn't cover or you didn't understand?

I'd look down at my little piece of scrap paper with a few notes scantily written out. I had learned to write my questions down as they popped into my head, then write the answers down after a phone call or a doctor's visit. Despite the fact that I had a spouse with a medical background, I felt it important to ask my own questions, to write my own answers down. The doctor had answered all those questions and inevitably, my mind would draw a blank for any more questions, and my head would shake no. Later, in the car, they would spill out like a bag of popcorn opened from the bottom end.

"How will she make her own ponytails?

"How will she hook a bra?

"How will she cut her meat?

"How will she dance with a boy with only one hand?"

"How, how, how?"

Accepting Rayna's disabilities alone was one hurdle; accepting her handicap in comparison to the other "normal" children was a mountain I have yet to climb over.

I'd volunteer to help at her Brownie troop; the girls would do an art project; I would help Rayna as she struggled to cut, paste, fold, string, tie, sew, or whatever "fun" task would be upon her. She would calmly, patiently, and diligently set about her task. The others would complete these tasks in half the time, with half the effort. They would ask Rayna if she needed help, and Rayna would proudly shake her head no. Rayna has her pride, and completing a task on her own is very important to her. She is never afraid to ask for help when she needs it.

"Can you tie my shoe?"

"Cut my meat?"

"I need help with..."

"Mommy, can you help me with..."

But if there were any way conceivable that Rayna could complete the task at hand independently, she would. I, on the other hand, would have more difficulty than she. I would look up, see the others deftly cutting, easily folding, as one hand held one side of the paper, and the other held the other. Rayna seemed unaffected by this, happily living in her own world.

Why couldn't I be more like her? Why was I so upset that she couldn't string the beads as easily as the others? She'd sit there humming, laboriously stringing, only asking for help when absolutely necessary, for independence was more important to her than anything. Why was I getting anxious and antsy?

I looked around at the others. I realized how angry I was. I thought about comparisons; how you sometimes don't realize how green an apple is until you put it in a basket with all red apples. I wanted my apple to turn red, to be like all the other apples. I didn't want Rayna to have to huff and puff to keep up with the norm. The first thing I needed to learn was to be able to look at Rayna and see the positive, see what she can accomplish, instead of what she can't do; look at how well she can walk, or even the fact that she is mobile, instead of how difficult her gait is. What I needed was a good dose of "practice what I preach."

I wish I had control; I wish I could make this disability go away. What also angered me was not controlling the things I was capable of controlling. Always at war with myself over my weight, I was the queen of the dieters. The irony is, I'm only about twenty pounds overweight, not massive, not obese, just perpetually frustrated. One would think it is such an easy formula.

One unhappy overweight human plus one careful nutrition plan equals one happy, perfect-weight individual human. But somehow, the mathematics never worked for me. I'd lose a few pounds, then sabotage myself with improper eating and never end up with the desired result. Besides being frustrated by this, I was in awe of its mystery. I couldn't understand how I could let something that I was in complete control over, control me. I can't climb in Rayna's head and remove her cavernous hemangioma and make her well, but I do have the power to lose twenty pounds. Ah, one of life's unsolved mysteries.

I remember sitting in one of those weight loss groups listening to the women explain why the scale went up that week. I had heard and experienced these thoughts so many times it almost became comical.

"I must be retaining water; it's that time of the month."

"I shouldn't have had that eensy-teensy piece of pie at Uncle Harry's birthday party." (I wondered why one eensy-teensy piece of pie made the scale tip three pounds in the upward direction.)

The only comment that I wanted to stand up and yell at the lady hit me so hard, I almost cried in recognizable fear. Her words definitely struck a chord.

"You don't understand the stress I'm under. I have more problems than I can deal with."

"Yeah, lady, like that extra piece of chocolate cake is going to make your problems go away," I laughed to myself. Never worked for me.

So, here I have control, and here I relinquish it to someone else. If only Rayna had the control over her illness, I bet she would be more successful with it than I.

"Like a suspended pendulum, not sure which way to swing." That was my way of describing Rayna. And other clichés.

"She falls between the cracks."

"Like a fish out of water."

"Invisible sorrow."

Rayna, like so many other children with mild to moderately severe disabilities, doesn't fit in any set category, any norm. They are not the developmentally delayed, the disabled, the "handicapped." They don't fit in the norm, and they don't fit in the "not norm." Like laundry drying outside on a windy day, they are blown in so many different directions, that you just can't catch it.

One of my favorite descriptions of Rayna is that she has a handicap—she is not handicapped. She stands in a corridor between two doors of life, neither locked to her, just difficult to enter. These doors became our way of life, always looking for the perfect way to fit into both, or either, not always sure which one was the best.

Another frustration I encountered in the course of Rayna's illness is what I so vividly describe as the "fillet of fish syndrome." As life settled into its everyday events and Rayna's world expanded, I realized that this world was not in on Rayna's illness from the start, was unaware of Rayna, and would need to know about Rayna in some capacity.

Rayna's new world encompassed new teachers, new friends, new friends' parents. With each addition, I knew I had to explain about Rayna, give them Rayna's story in "twenty words" or less, an overview of her life, squish all the horrors into a few short sentences, so that they would be aware of her infirmities, have an understanding of how "to help her with the things that can not be helped by Rayna herself." I would have to tell them that her right hand was weakened, that she needed help on the stairs, help putting on her coat, help cutting food, help doing any art projects, help here, help there, help everywhere...I began to feel like a fish fillet, opening my soul to the world, letting everyone know "what was going on with Rayna." In retrospect, what I really needed was a book, Rayna's manual, a guide to dealing with Rayna.

We continued our yearly visits to Duke, always settling on the Labor Day weekend as the optimum time to travel and see Dr. DeLong. After a few years of steady, positive MRIs without any further incidence of bleeding, I began to "relax" a little about these visits. The usual anticipation anxieties that always occurred before MRI checkups started to dissipate. I became expectant of only good results and started looking at these MRI tests as routine—"just to make sure everything is status quo." I started letting my guard down.

When the "call" came, the Duke to Newton long distance call, the one we always received a few days after the visit, the "everything was fine as usual, see you next year" call, I casually sat in the kitchen as Allyn spoke to the doctor. When "Great, good to hear it" was replaced with "I see," "Yes, I understand," and "When would you want to do this?" the inevitable panic flashed through my body.

This year's MRI had revealed that Rayna's lesion had

increased in size. Theories? Rayna had grown, so the blood vessels had grown. Or, the other possibility—it really isn't vascular after all, but a slow-growing tumor. Next on Rayna's dance card? A PET scan. A what? A positive emission tomagraphy. Once again, a new test had emerged on the scene, which would confirm once and for all whether this was vascular or not. A radioactive dye would be injected into Rayna's brain. She would then have to lie perfectly still on the examining table while the physical metabolism of the lesion could be traced.

Since the residue of the dye lingered for six to eight hours, it was imperative to keep Rayna apart from Tovah, since Tovah was a child and more susceptible to negative effects of the radioactive material. Because it was new, only one hospital had this test in Boston and they weren't prepared yet to perform it on children under the age of eighteen. A hospital in New York already had it in service, but so did Duke. Thus, we decided we would just go back to Duke, familiar territory.

Landing at the Raleigh/Durham airport felt strange. A land returned to, yet not like our traditional Labor Day. The air was different, the vegetation different, the easygoing feeling I had experienced weeks before was also different, in fact gone. There is something to be said about change in life, spontaneity, breaking out of routine; but right now, I would have opted for safe, reliable, and predictable.

Two wonderful results came out of this off-season visit to our medical home away from home. The first being, once and for all, forever and ever more, I never had to worry that this was a malignant tumor that could grow in Rayna's head. With definite precision and assurance, this new test confirmed that what was invading Rayna's head (and life) could only be vascular. Her growth as a human being had taken the cavernous hemangioma right along with it. Rayna grew, it grew. Now, I could go back to my "normal" life of daily worrying that it might bleed again. Perspectives really can play havoc with your mind.

The other result was one of those unbelievable bump into,

find a blast from the past in the least likely place, experiences.

We needed to check in for a quick visit with Dr. DeLong just prior to the test. While waiting for him, the girls and I wandered to the snack bar. Upon our return, we noticed Allyn was talking to some people who looked familiar. Upon approach, my mouth dropped open as I realized it was a classmate of Allyn's from dental school. We had been friendly throughout the four years but had lost touch over the last decade. We hugged, reuniting, and felt like two aliens on a planet who knew no one else. Monica, the wife, quickly filled me in on the details of how they bumped into Allyn. Awaiting an appointment with her daughter, she wandered into the waiting room and noticed Allyn sitting there. She returned to the examination room to her husband.

"Dan, it's uncanny, there's a guy out in the waiting room who is the spitting image of your friend Allyn from dental school."

Curious, Dan went to the waiting room, discovered Allyn, and returned to the examination room to retrieve Monica.

"Monica, dear, that guy doesn't just look like Allyn. It is Allyn."

You never know where you'll discover people in life, and you never know how tragedy can strike so many people in the world. Sometimes, I'll stand in a crowd at an event, scan the people around me and be curious about their stories. What happiness has been bestowed upon them? What tragedies have befallen them? What loved ones have died in their lives? Everyone has stories, everyone has baggage, it's just a question of the balance.

And Monica and Dan, too, have had their balance upset. They were there for a crucial tell-all exam as well. They were going to find out if the leukemia that had plagued their eleven-year-old five years earlier was still in remission. We wished each other well, standing isolated in the hall together, a common bond, a common tragedy, promising to get together the next Labor Day. (Their travel time to Duke consisted of a twenty-minute car ride. They had settled in Chapel Hill!)

They say it's a small world. Times like this make that expression ring true. The two families left Duke that day clinging to the words of our respective doctors who had bestowed welcome results on our daughters. We left with successful news and a renewed friendship.

So, life goes on…in Massachusetts and North Carolina.

Life settled back into its routine, the latest scare behind us, the "army" prepared in case… The "in case" came in a form I never could have dreamed would be part of our agenda in life. And as "prepared" as I thought I was to handle anything, any challenge, I wasn't, and wasn't in a big way.

It had been a typical day, school for the girls, work for Allyn, exercise, domestic tasks, and some writing for me. Nighttime came with the usual bedtime rituals so familiar to childhood. Tovah had just fallen asleep. Allyn was in Rayna's room checking on her when he heard a strange noise coming out of Tovah's room. He immediately went in to find Tovah sitting up in her bed in a seizure. He screamed for me to come in as the seizure finished, having only lasted thirty to sixty seconds. Once assured it was over, he had me sit with her while he dialed the hospital. A wonderful friend, Harriet, came over to stay with Rayna, who had remained asleep, and we rushed Tovah to Children's Hospital. Familiar place, familiar sounds, familiar everything except, not the usual child. Frightened beyond belief, I sat with Tovah, an arm protectively tightened around her, as if I could shield her from harm, like I tried to shield Rayna. The doctor examined her and assured us that she was in no immediate danger; everything checked out okay. We were allowed to take her home for the night, but we had to return the next day for an EEG.

Tovah was diagnosed with a childhood disorder called Benign Rolandic Epilepsy of Childhood, and the words spoke their explanations. It was benign; it would only last through childhood with an anticipation of puberty as its cessation time. For the most part, these kinds of seizures could only occur nocturnally. She would wake up into them. For the next four years, Tovah was intermittently on control medicine, routinely checked with EEGs and clinical exams, and experienced less than half a dozen seizures. With much good fortune she has totally outgrown this disease. We take our positives with baby steps and thank God for every one we take.

As with Rayna, my heart broke for Tovah—for the uncertainty of her medical condition, for the vulnerability she had to experience with such a disease. We are all subject to many things by being placed on this earth, including uncertainty. There are just some times in our lives when we find ourselves in more precarious states than other times. Having one child plagued with an illness didn't preclude having another afflicted. We were never given any guarantees that just because one family member was stricken with a medical problem, the rest of us would be immune. In retrospect, I think I subconsciously believed in that concept. Although statistically, the problems plaguing one family aren't always a multitude, we are not given any magic formula in life that limits our problems; no magic number for the amount of traumas we encounter on our journey of life. Rayna's illness did not guarantee Tovah would never be sick, nor Allyn or me. We can only hope for the best in life, do our best to protect ourselves from the negative elements that may befall us, yet we can't live in constant fear, constantly looking over our shoulders. I celebrate Tovah's total recovery and once again remind myself that nothing should ever be taken for granted. Nothing.

So, for Tovah, life goes on.

As Rayna progressed more in academics, plunging into the early elementary grades, some weaknesses in her learning became apparent to her teacher. Rayna was not learning at the rate targeted for her age. The area in which this was most noticeable was reading; Rayna was not reading; she couldn't decode the words; she had word retrieval loss, and a host of other disabilities started to surface. A new area of testing was now necessary—not CAT scans, or MRIs, or arteriograms, but neuropsychology, reading aptitude tests, WISC-R, learning center coordinators' assessments, etc.

Rayna's disabilities now crossed the path from just medical to academic as well. How utterly frustrating. To speak to Rayna, to have a conversation with her, one would think one was talking to an adult. Her level of sophistication, her expanded vocabulary, put her in a realm far beyond her years. Yet, sitting at a desk in school, she was struggling. Another area for Rayna to be different was now upon her. Luckily, learning disabilities these days seem to be readily noticed, readily diagnosed, and readily addressed. Rayna was evaluated, a special education plan put in place for her, and the road to education was made smoother for her.

So, for Rayna's education, life goes on.

When Rayna was seven, a disaster hit our community, our group of friends. A tragedy happened to two very good friends. Their eight-year-old daughter was diagnosed with a malignant brain tumor and within the time span of one week, she died. I cried for days, I spent sleepless nights. My heart ached for my friends, for their older daughter, for me, for my family. I went to the funeral with a heavy heart, wishing that my prayers, my hopes, anything could will this child back to life. I couldn't imagine a tragedy so devastating. The funeral housed many families crying for the tragedy, mourning for the child, the loss, the injustice of an eight-year-old being shut off from life so young. We cried, and when we thought we couldn't cry anymore, we cried some more.

We all went home that day, hugging our own children just a little bit harder, just a little bit longer, and somehow that day, it really didn't seem all that important whether the Legos got put away or not.

Both girls had a lot of difficulty dealing with this trauma, Rayna especially. She experienced sudden fear for herself; maybe that unconscious awareness that surfaces eventually in our lives, the realization of everyone's mortality and vulnerability, had come to the surface in whatever way it comes for a seven-year-old. With the wonderful help of the child psychologist we got through this.

And life goes on.

The unexpected medical implications of all of this were overwhelming. A year later, when Rayna was eight years old, she had a routine visit to the endocrinologist. Rayna had been seeing this doctor since she was diagnosed, since the bleed was in the thalamus and near the pituitary. On this particular visit, he expressed some concern to me that she was falling off the charts in weight and height and her growth had slowed down. He was concerned that the bleed had impeded her growth hormone capabilities, that she might possibly not grow any taller than the little over four feet she already was. He felt the best thing to do at this point was to admit her to the hospital overnight for a specialized test that had to be done while she was sleeping. I sure hoped whatever roommate she had this time, the mother was a *Sesame Street* fan. As it turned out, because a nurse would be monitoring Rayna all night, a private room was a necessity. Thank goodness for the little luxuries in life.

Rayna didn't need to be admitted until noontime. She had told our rabbi at services the week before that she was going to be in the hospital. Rayna, so endearing, always develops beautiful relationships with people, both children and adults. The combination of one warm, compassionate eight-year-old and one warm, compassionate rabbi made for a wonderful relationship. The morning before we left for the hospital, the telephone rang and it was Rabbi Yellin to speak with Rayna. He wished her well and best of luck. I automatically assumed from this phone call that he was unable to visit Rayna in the hospital and was making a phone call to her in lieu of his visit.

Rayna was admitted around noon, given the usual pre-op exam, now something I was quite familiar with. She cut and pasted a glitter project in the playroom with the recreational therapist and was not there more than thirty minutes, when she looked up to see Rabbi Yellin walking down the corridor towards the playroom to visit her. What a wonderful human being.

Rayna ate supper, then bravely sat on the examining table, clutching her panda bear, as I put my arm around her shoulder while the IV was placed in her hand. When she went to sleep, the nurse would come in every fifteen minutes for the next eight hours to take blood from her. Because hormones for growth are manufactured at night during the sleep cycle, this would determine where Rayna was in her growth cycle.

Rayna's number of hospital admissions was growing and her hospital chart was getting thicker. It was decided that this time Allyn would stay with Rayna and I would go home with Tovah. I kissed Rayna good-night, hugged her with a force of strength I didn't know possible, then stood at the elevator feeling like I had abandoned my daughter, unsuccessfully endeavoring to hide my tears. But, I was lucky. I was with someone who understood, even if she was only ten years old. She had an insight to my emotions, to my worries, and she put her hand in mine and whispered, "It's okay, Mommy."

I was lucky. I was going home with Tovah. We would snuggle in bed together, keep each other company, help each other "get through the night." I was going home to take care of Tovah and she was going to take care of me. Boy, do I love my children, admire them, and cherish each and every day with them.

A few weeks later, the results of this test were ready and the doctor explained to us that indeed his suspicions were confirmed. Rayna was not growing. The bleed had done damage to the growth cycle, and Rayna wouldn't grow any taller unless she was given growth hormone medication. Rayna would need a daily injection of growth hormone and once again, because the body cycle has its growth time during sleep, the optimum time for administering this would be just before bedtime. He explained that the medicine would be delivered to us once a month, needed refrigeration, and would come in two vials, one powder, one liquid, and we would mix it up, since once it was mixed it was only good for about ten days. Therefore, several powder vials and several liquid vials would be delivered. Also, syringes would be delivered as well as a medical waste receptacle. We would also need alcohol wipes. I listened to all this with my head swimming as Allyn casually nodded, absorbing it all with the ease of someone in the medical profession. The doctor asked if I had any questions, and I asked if he really wanted to make it home by dinner that night. Home nursing services were available to train us, but I told him I would observe Allyn and learn from him and then if there were any questions, I'd call him back.

And oh, yes there was one other thing about this medicine that we needed to know. Without it Rayna would not grow. With it, she would.

Oh, yes, one more thing, again. There was a chance our medical insurance would not cover it.

The medicine cost three thousand dollars a month.

As it turned out, our insurance did pay for it. The first batch was delivered a few days later. I sat and watched as Allyn easily and deftly mixed up the batches, explaining that I needed to know all this in case he was out of town or working late. Then it hit me; Allyn was not going to be the only one administering this shot. This was something I needed to learn and learn fast. The first few nights Allyn gave the injection, and, true to form, Rayna took it with all the courage she has taken everything else, with hardly a complaint.

Then the inevitable came. The girls and I were going to Cape Cod for a few days to visit friends. Realizing this, I knew the time had come to learn. I was so frightened of taking a needle and injecting it into Rayna's skin. But, I knew that my fears couldn't be stronger than my need to take care of Rayna and, more importantly, of Rayna's need to be taken care of by me.

"You'll practice on an orange," Allyn reassured me.

Somehow, I knew all the practice on an orange, grapefruit, whatever inanimate object, was not going to have the same impact as actually giving a shot to my own flesh and blood. I don't love an orange and cry for that orange when it is hurt.

When the time came to actually give Rayna the shot, I knew if I was ever going to be as brave as Rayna is in life, then I had better march into her room with all the bravery one person could conjure up and give my daughter her shot, her growth, her hope.

I stood there looking from the needle to the skin, the skin to the needle, and knew it had to be done. I took a deep breath, inserted the needle, and the most amazing thing happened. The sky didn't fall down. The needle slid into her skin and I watched in utter amazement as the liquid disappeared. Allyn watched with approving silence, like a parent proudly watching a child at a piano recital, nodding to the beat of the song. Rayna didn't scream, in fact, the silence in the room was ominous. The only loud thundering noise in the room was my heart pounding.

Rayna, being the wonderfully nurturing child that she is, only gave me accolades on my achievement, rave reviews of my debut, and said how proud she was of me. How did I deserve such a wonderful daughter?

I marched out of the room, amazed at this major accomplishment, proud of my success, proud of overcoming this hurdle, and proud that I could finally be an active healer in Rayna's illness, at least medically. Then it struck, what I had just accomplished and how very frightened I was. I started to cry and cry and cry and kept crying. I cried for everything, for all the injustices, for all the anger and frustration, for all the years ahead and what other unexpected obstacles were going to be put in her path.

I'm known as the optimistic one, but that night, I had a lot of difficulty living up to that reputation. Giving Rayna that first shot was one of the hardest things I have ever done in my life.

And life goes on.

Shortly after that, the orthopedic surgeon announced that Rayna would greatly benefit from an operation called a tendon transfer where the tendons from the stronger muscles would be transposed so that Rayna would be better able to manipulate her hand function. Only a few months after the endocrine hospitalization, Rayna once again returned to Children's Hospital to have this tendon transfer on her right wrist and forearm. This time we thought about asking for a private room, but decided that a roommate might be a positive experience, now that Rayna was older. She could benefit from another child to talk to and share similar experiences. Her roommate was lovely (as well as the mother).

And life goes on.

A few months after that, the orthopedic surgeon felt that she had done so well with the hand that the leg might benefit from a similar operation, so Rayna had a leg operation, a calcaneal osteotomy, and a heel cord lengthening to help with mobility of her foot and ankle.

For six weeks after the surgery she could not put any pressure on her leg, thus, a wheelchair was in order. So, for six weeks, I entered another dimension of Rayna's life as her mobility was now confined to a wheelchair. My whole life centered around ensuring Rayna's mobility. I got a firsthand look at how very difficult life is for those permanently confined to this means of transportation.

She would be picked up for school by one of those vans that lowers the lift, wheels the person onto the lift, lifts them in the car and transports them in the car in the wheelchair. When the van came for the first time, I panicked that Rayna would be frightened in that little ride up into the van. As the van lifted her up, I held my breath and then heard Rayna go, "wee" and laugh. She had several wonderful drivers. The first day she was to return to school was upon us, and I felt that feeling of abandoment once again. Her first driver was Bob, a friendly, fatherly type, who dealt with these kinds of situations all the time. He was chitchatty and compassionate, and I felt better that Rayna was in good hands. After all she was being driven six-tenths of a mile up the street.

Another life lesson. My panic time could probably be reduced by fifty percent if I just relaxed a little and waited for the situation to unfold. Put that on my list to discuss with the psychologist.

These six weeks included her birthday. On the actual day of her birthday, it was pouring—not just raining—but a real "cats and dogs" rain. But we were not going to spoil Rayna's celebration at the restaurant she chose to go to. A cousin of Allyn's once said it so true. "So, because it's raining, does that mean the world stops? Just changes a little."

We drove to the restaurant of her choice, and Allyn pulled up to the door. I hopped out, pulled the wheelchair out of the car, quickly got it opened up, wheeled it right next to the car door, wiped it with a towel, opened an umbrella to hold over her head, helped Rayna slide her body into the chair, as Tovah helped me cover the cast with a garbage bag, and quickly wheeled her into the restaurant to celebrate. After all, we were celebrating nine years of life.

The day the doctor said she could put pressure on her leg, and spend a few hours a day out of the wheelchair, is one of the more memorable etched in my memory. Two significant events stand out in my mind. The first was her flying-up ceremony from Brownies to Girl Scouts.

We arrived at the leader's house, full of excitement, with that special family-outing feeling. Allyn carried the still camera, I was carrying the VCR, and Tovah carried the flowers. This seemed to be our standard attire whenever one child was experiencing a significant event in life.

A makeshift wooden bridge was set up so the girls could walk the bridge, starting out as a Brownie on one side and ending up as a Girl Scout on the other. My heart sank; I knew Rayna, for the umpteenth time in her life, was going to experience an event in an alternative fashion. So many times in her life, her accomplishments are carried out differently; things are slightly adjusted for Rayna and just a slight bit different from the way I ever anticipated when I carried her for nine months.

The ceremony began, and as each girl was called to walk across, my heart beat faster, broke a little more. The leader had told Rayna not to be concerned, that it would be very special for her to walk next to the bridge. She was understanding and tender about Rayna, but nothing could insulate my disappointed feelings. I suppose I should have just been grateful that she could even walk a little that night, that the wheelchair got left home by itself in the darkened living room, abandoned for the night as Rayna started walking again.

Rayna's name was called. I took a deep breath, blinked back the tears, and the most miraculous thing happened. Unbeknownst to me, Rayna had engaged the help of one of her fellow troop members and, incredulously, was walking across the bridge as the whole room exploded in a thunderous applause. I could hardly see this happening, my eyes were so blurry from tears, but there she was, holding her head up high, slowly inching her way across the bridge. She definitely gives validity to the word courage.

The next day, I was to return the wheelchair, the second significant event I remember from that time. I drove to the equipment rental place, wheeled the empty chair into the office, and walked out crying. I cried for relief that with all of Rayna's problems, I thanked God that this was only a temporary situation, that my daughter could walk, and run, be it with an uneven gait, but she could walk. My heart poured out to all the people whose wheelchairs are their permanent means of mobility and who will never be able to walk. I was truly getting an education on how to put life into perspective.

And so I returned the wheelchair. And Rayna walked again.

And life goes on.

One day yet another year later, as Rayna was approaching her tenth birthday, she declared that the lefties of the world should be recognized and that there should be a day to honor lefties. The doctors had determined that Rayna would most likely have been a righty, but was a "forced" lefty due to the bleed.

"How come they have a Mother's Day and a Father's Day, but there is no day to honor lefties?"

I listened to Rayna's request and told her that perhaps the governor could declare a lefties day. Without any further ado, with Allyn's help, she wrote a letter to Governor William Weld and told him her story and her request for a day to honor lefties.

"Dear Governor Weld…I am writing to you because…I think you can do something to help people like myself…I was hoping that you...so that people like myself could feel special instead of just being different...I know that you are a very busy person...Thank you very much..."

Shortly after that, she received a telephone call from the governor's office and sure enough, a lefties' day was going to be declared that year. They were going to make it on May 29—Rayna's birthday.

On the appointed day of the reading of the declaration, we dressed up in our "Sunday best" and headed to the governor's office. (The governor was called away unexpectedly, so the lieutenant governor did the honors.) What a proud day. We smiled brightly for the photographers, exchanged firm handshakes with important officials, and added a dimension to the children's life experiences, something to tell their children, their grandchildren.

We all reveled in Rayna's accomplishment. This was truly her moment in time. Part of our family bonding, part of our family strength, is to always try our best to be together for important occasions, to "be there" for everyone's "moments in time," for Tovah's ballet recitals, soccer games, plays at school. This is the solid foundation that helps build the continuity in our family, the substance of our family, our nucleus. We are together. We are each other's cheering squad.

Rayna has a heart filled with such love and concern for her fellow man. She wanted to see lefties honored so she did something about it. She makes things happen. She moves things. She moves me.

She moves me—what an understatement. Somewhere along the line in the years following Rayna's diagnosis, we became attached to the song, "Wind Beneath My Wings," especially after seeing the movie *Beaches*. It became our song. Rayna, in my eyes, is a hero, not just a hero, but heroic as well. She is someone I model myself after when looking for inner strength and courage.

To endure all that Rayna has faced with the amount of courage that she exhibits puts her on my hero list.

So, for Rayna, my hero, life goes on.

And just as the actor thanks the people behind the scenes, I too think of other types of heroes. Being the sibling of a child with medical problems and special needs is challenging, frustrating, and difficult. "Special siblings," I've heard them called. I call Tovah more than a special sibling. I call her a hero, too.

So, for Tovah, my heroic daughter, my other teacher, life goes on.

I am the mother and they are the daughters, yet I draw strength from them. I look at Rayna's courageous actions, her heroic bravery and truly feel she is the wind beneath my wings. Whenever I am in any uncomfortable situation, having an annual checkup with blood tests, for example, I close my eyes as the technician puts the needle in, and tell myself that if Rayna can go through all that she has to endure, I can be brave, too. It's a wonderful world when a mother can learn from her daughters, when a mother can be thankful for all the things in life that her daughters have taught her.

And life goes on.

Chapter Five

THE ENEMY WAS BACK

As the seventh year of being "bleed free" approached, I truly believed we were out of the woods, that every year that went by with Rayna's condition remaining stable was a sign that everything was going to be okay, that she would never bleed again. Looking back, I don't know now if that is what I honestly believed or only what I willed myself to believe.

So life calmed down with just its routine physical exams, weekly physical therapy, psychology visits, nightly shots, etc., etc., etc. I was lulled into a sense of security, a sense that the worst was over, despite the fact that I knew that Rayna's condition was precarious, with no guarantees. I felt temporarily safe.

After all, this was the seventh year, and the number seven has associated with it some positive and fun identifications.

Lucky seven, seventh inning stretch, seven years of good luck. Of course, also associated with that is seven years of bad luck; break a mirror, seven years of bad luck are upon you. I don't believe in that or any other superstitions. I never throw salt over my shoulder, knock on wood, avoid black cats in my path; I just live my life, trying to control the things I can, and trying not to be a helpless victim to the things I can't be the commander in chief over.

But, there it was, the seven years of "good health," of the blood vessels being good, of not damaging Rayna's life anymore, and as all that came to an end, I found my sense of temporary security that I was lulled into was nothing more than the calm before the storm.

Like the broken mirror, Rayna's seven years of "remission" was shattered, as was my sense of well-being. I have found it hard to ever trust anything stable in life again.

It was with that peace of mind, that false sense of security, that Rayna and I boarded a plane to California for a week of visiting friends, relatives and some business in Los Angeles related to my script writing. Tovah was off at overnight camp in Maine and had chosen to stay there instead of the trip.

Rayna and Tovah are both experienced travelers with the worldly sophistication that comes from broadening your geographic horizons. Rayna, quite adept at carrying on conversations with adults in a sophisticated fashion, was having a wonderful conversation with a man seated next to her. He showed her pictures of his little girl, and she talked about her love of seeing the Rocky Mountains from a plane, how it gives her a sense of wonder.

As the plane approached the San Francisco airport, I suggested that Rayna do some of her hand exercises as she talked to the man. She started to open and close her fist for her first exercise and abandoned it before one completion with the declaration that she'll do it later. I didn't push her on this since we were on vacation. I would have her do them later. Later never came.

We awoke on our first morning in California looking

forward to a walk on the Golden Gate Bridge, a stroll through Ghiradelli Square, devouring their famous hot fudge sundaes, followed by coffee and sourdough bread, a favorite food of ours. As we were getting ready for the day, Rayna told me her right hand felt funny. Although that momentary instant of panic struck my heart, I calmly reassured her that it was probably the way she slept.

That's another "issue" with having a child with an illness. You never know what is wrong due to the condition; if she really slept wrong on her arm or if the enemy is back.

We started out on what was to be our marvelous day of sightseeing, but I knew something was wrong. She seemed to walk slower, move slower, and all around was not the same child as the day before. That wonderful lesson I gave myself of reducing my panic by fifty percent was buried somewhere in my brain, and, for the life of me, I couldn't bring it to the foreground; that old adage how only a mother knows her own child is the only thought that was surfacing. As much as I didn't want to believe it, I knew something had clearly changed in Rayna, and I had a heavy, ominous feeling this was not a change for the better.

We stopped at the Golden Gate Bridge first. We walked out onto the bridge, staring at the breathtaking view below us, thanking God for all his splendor, for giving us this world, for the sparkling water, the milky white clouds, the magnificent rock formations...How could anything be wrong with Rayna if we could stand here amidst this perfect scene?

We smiled at the camera as our friends took a picture. Later, when I returned home and had the pictures developed, I noticed Rayna was the only one with a genuine smile. My smile was forced, contrived, made up, obscured by the fear that something was not right, "something," such a generic word can mean so much. In this case, something translated into nightmare.

I called Allyn, told him my observations. He called me back, told me the results of his checking with the doctors. There was a slight possibility that Rayna was "leaking out," the blood vessels were bleeding. Since she wasn't showing any emergency signs, and since no major decision would be made in the next few days, I should stay there and finish out the trip.

"There's no real reason to spoil the trip for her." Allyn's words couldn't have rung truer. I have always put my children's welfare before any of my own needs. Some sacrifices have been minimal and some have been ones that to this day, I wonder how I ever endured them.

The next six days were a joy to Rayna and a nightmare to me. This clearly didn't come under the heading of "minimal sacrifice." The days dragged by with dread, dread that I had to "be on" for Rayna, not to let her into my little world of fear and apprehension. I needed to keep her in her world of experiencing a trip to California that would long be remembered with fond memories. I didn't want to believe that this was happening to her. She had come so far, so much therapy, so many operations, so much rebuilding. I didn't want the tower to crumble. I wanted that pot of gold so badly, and if I couldn't have that, I certainly didn't want to turn around and go backwards.

The rest of the trip was a wonderful memory for Rayna and a blur of images to me. Pier 39, Half Moon Bay, Carmel, Monterey, Chinatown, Lombard Street, "doing lunch" with a producer. My body went through all the motions as my heart sank further. My doubts and suspicions about Rayna were now affirmations. I could no longer fool myself any longer, shut my eyes and wish it weren't true, for when I opened my eyes, reality was there to greet me.

I once wrote a children's book about a little turtle with a crooked shell. He wasn't very happy about his crooked shell. Every morning the turtle would play his "game." Standing in front of a mirror, he would close his eyes and recite:

Mirror, mirror, when I open my eyes,
Please show me a magic surprise.
For what I would like to see,
Is a shell as straight as can be.

But, each day, when the turtle opened his eyes, the mirror always showed the same thing. The mirror always won the game.

Wouldn't it be nice if we did possess magical powers, if we could will things the way we wanted them to be, just by snapping our fingers, waving magic wands, saying, "abracadabra." Unfortunately, God didn't give us these powers. But, he gave me Rayna, and with it the strength to fight for her, her health, her life. And I was going to need all the strength in the world to face what the next few months would bring.

By the time we reached the San Diego Zoo, it was so tiresome for Rayna to walk around, we decided that a wheelchair would make it more comfortable. We put her in a wheelchair, and she had a fun-filled day watching the animals, enjoying the world. My uncle pushed her. I walked next to her.

Rayna watched monkeys scratching, swinging from limb to limb, lions stealthily pacing, birds flying, elephants swaying their trunks, exclaiming "oohs" and "aahs," "how cute," "how adorable." I watched the people. It's amazing how people stop to look at anyone different. I would wonder what these people were thinking when they looked at Rayna being wheeled around a zoo in a wheelchair; pity? curiosity?

Why were they staring at her? When she was in the wheelchair after the leg surgery with a cast covered with "Good luck Rayna," "Break a leg Rayna," "Lori was here," "Get better soon," written in every color of the rainbow, it looked like a broken leg to the public and was accepted with that premise.

"Oh, look at the little girl. She must have broken her leg."

"Oh, my, how did you break your leg, little girl?"

It's not a broken leg. I had a tendon transfer and a heel cord replacement along with a calcaneal osteotomy due to my right hemiparesis because of my cavernous hemangioma in the left thalamus that bled. Any other questions?

"I'm the star quarterback for my football team and I fell."

"Skiing."

"Rollerblading."

"I fell down off the jungle gym."

These were the answers, if given, that would get the nods, the assents, the identifiable, the unpitied stares. The cast was her external message to the world that, "Hey, I'm okay, folks, just your normal kid, with no cares in the world, who broke my leg." This could have been our standard answer, how succinct, how encapsulated.

But, at the San Diego Zoo, there was no cast to serve as her protective barrier, to tell the world that she's otherwise normal. The stares were looks of pity, raised eyebrows in curiosity, stares of sympathy, followed by whispering to the person next to them.

Intellectually, I understood. We are all curious about anything that sticks out from the norm. If thirty people enter a room and one wears a hat, that's the person most stared at, most thought about, most likely to pique our curiosity. I am just as much a victim of this. Emotionally, I was angry, I wanted to be left alone, to get through this "fun" day at the zoo, to fly home, to be engulfed in Allyn's arms, reassuring me she'd be okay, to shut my eyes to these onlookers, to have Rayna look in the mirror and have the mirror lose the game.

I've had that frustrating feeling many times before. To help Rayna with her leg weakness, she occasionally wears a leg brace. When she has pants on, there are no stares, but if she wears it with shorts in the warm weather, I'll notice a few stares. Again—curiosity? pity? I think of all the people who walk around with braces on their teeth. These too are noticed by people, but there is a difference between being noticed and being stared at. But why? Aren't these two kinds of braces doing similar things to the body? One is straightening teeth and one is strengthening a leg. Why then is someone with a leg brace more visibly set apart from the norm than someone with braces on her teeth?

The plane ride home felt like six days instead of six hours. It seemed endless. I found myself choking back the tears, staring out the window, looking at endless clouds. I have no real fear of flying, always looking at it is as an escape, high up above the world, the crisp blue sky, clouds that look like marshmallows, but on this trip, I felt like a prisoner trapped in my seat as friendly stewardesses endeavored to cater to our every need and want. Unfortunately, my needs and wants at this time were not going to be met by someone dispensing peanuts, coffee, tea, or juice, and smiles a mile long.

The inevitable happened at the airport. Rayna had to be told. She needed to know that she was going to have a CAT scan, to see why her hand was so weak, why she was having so much trouble walking. Allyn sat with Rayna as I waited for the luggage. I watched the bags go around. I looked back at Rayna, Allyn's hand gently around her shoulder. I watched the bags go around. I looked back and saw Rayna nodding sadly. I watched the bags go around. I looked back and saw Allyn gently rubbing Rayna's hand. I watched the bags go around. I looked back and saw Rayna dabbing at her eyes, then she looked up at me, meeting my eyes, with a look of understanding well beyond her years, her big brown eyes so sad as she clutched her panda bear. The bags came and made their way around the carousel a few times. Allyn got up to help me carry them. It was time to go home.

We were loaded down with souvenirs, T-shirts, ticket stubs, key chains proudly displaying Hollywood symbols, San Diego animals—all the signs of a happy, carefree vacation.

At nine o'clock the next morning, a CAT scan delivered to me the only souvenir I recall of this vacation. Rayna had bled again.

The enemy was back.

Chapter Six

NO-CHOICE CHOICES

The head I had been holding so high the last seven years now hung low. I was devastated. If I had questioned it the first time, I had no tolerance for it the second time. I couldn't believe this could happen again. I truly had believed or made myself believe it would never happen again.

I must have been the biggest optimist. Allyn, on the other hand, the family's resident pessimist, kept pacing the house, thanking God that it wasn't a worse bleed than it was. He was (although as equally upset) relieved at its mildness, its nonseverity. This was a time when seeing the glass always half empty gave him a protective coating from the hurt. He has always believed in never expecting the good in life and then you won't be disappointed. I always saw the sunshine on a cloudy day, for I knew the clouds may be covering it, but somewhere underneath was sunshine. My glass was always half full. This time, he was better prepared with his philosophies, his protective barriers.

I decided to go talk to my parents. They were always there for me, and I knew I could draw strength from them now. So, I took a ride and parked my car. Somehow, visiting the cemetery right now gave me a sense of peace, that feeling when you were young and thought that your parents could make all the bad things go away and protect you from all the evils in life. So, I talked to my parents, thought about how young they were to die, my mother, sixty-nine, my father, sixty-eight. I looked over at my grandmother's grave; she died in her nineties. I thought about my friend's daughter, dying at age eight.

I thought about the expression, "at least he lived a long life." I wonder who determines long. When a child dies, what do you say? At least they got through diapers, finished toddlerhood? Or is it more anguish for a parent burying a child, because when a parent dies, the offspring feels saddened and upset, but at least this is the "natural" course of life. But when a parent loses a child, there are the feelings of wondering how someone you brought into this world could leave you before you do. Is it because they had "their time," they finished their childhood, finished their adolescence, just didn't finish their adulthood, but then again, what is the finish to an adulthood? Is it fifty? sixty? seventy? eighty? ninety? one hundred and still going strong? Or are there no gradations assigned to anguish? Death is death. I don't know.

I feel so responsible. I chose to bring her into this world, to give her life, and I feel this overwhelming responsibility to help her keep this life—with quality and dignity. But then I ask, does that responsibility ever end? And I know the answer.

The next few weeks brought tests, examinations, numerous phone calls to doctors, radiologists, surgeons, more sleepless nights, more tears, more of everything that we had experienced almost seven years before, only I didn't want to see any reviews of this event. Once had been more than enough.

"Let's look at the MRI again."

"Sandy and Allyn, it may be time to consider intervention."

"Sandy, are you sure nothing unusual happened in California—a fall, car accident, anything?"

"Yes, something happened, Doctor; I left my heart in San Francisco...and San Diego...and L.A...and everywhere."

What to do next perplexed the team of doctors, and the team kept growing as the decision needed to be made. Rayna's case was a true puzzle to these doctors; there were no magic solutions, no volumes of text with clear-cut answers, no flipping to the index to look up Rayna's condition, turning back to the page to tell it all. The old horse race was about to start again. Radiate? Operate? Leave Alone? I had no interest in putting my bets on any of these horses...I wanted miracles and I wanted them now.

Rayna's strength started to return—"spontaneous recovery." The doctors kept meeting, conferring, comparing notes, x-rays, findings. Because of the invasive nature of any medical intervention, whether radiation or surgery, the decision-making procedure took time, yet there was one teensy sliver of light. The bleed had been minor, perhaps intense observation might be the answer and no intervention may be necessary, the *laissez-faire* approach again.

This ever-growing team of neurologists, surgeons, radiologists, and neuroradiologists had scheduled a meeting to make a final decision on the next course to follow in treating Rayna. Two days prior to the meeting, almost eight weeks after the "California bleed," Rayna had a third bleed, not a minor bleed, but an all-out massive bleed. In its devastating wake, it left behind double vision, a weakened leg and hand, and this time facial paralysis. Rayna now drooled out of her right side of the mouth, having absolutely no feeling there. And that was only the external damage.

The bleed had wiped out Rayna, my energy, my

hope...Vocabulary words such as "possibly," "perhaps," were now replaced with "definites," "musts," "have to's" all leading to one inevitable conclusion: new choices had to be made. No-choice choices, the easiest kind—the hardest kind. Choosing plastic or paper at the supermarket would have been the preferred dilemma of the day.

Rayna's world seemed to be crumbling before my very eyes. As we sat in the doctor's office, we listened to the alternatives. Surgery or radiation. Radiation or surgery. Leave Alone was left in the dust, not even a contender in this race for life. The neurosurgeon felt very strongly that the malformation could be resected with surgery, but in his words, "there'd be a seventy percent chance of wrecking Rayna."

Another new possibility would be to do a radically different kind of radiation, a proton beam radiation. This would be more precise in hitting the affected area and possibly not damaging to other areas around the malformation. There was just one major consideration for this type of radiation. It had never been done before for this type of lesion in this location.

The proton beam radiation has been in use for about forty years treating various kinds of problems, but there was never a case like Rayna's. Therefore, if we went ahead with this treatment, Rayna would be a test case for this kind of radiation for her kind of problem.

The doctor looked at me as I sat there wringing a handkerchief, constantly dabbing at my eyes. He compassionately asked me what my biggest fear was. I hesitated in answering. It was a tie—a tie between Rayna dying or Rayna living, but living with no life, a "vegetable." I honestly didn't know which fear was worse. I did know that I would do anything humanly possible to "get my Rayna back," the child so full of life and hope.

This radiation had never been done before, so we had absolutely nothing to compare it to: no success stories of how it has successfully cured this problem before, no comparisons of long-term results, no textbook jargon of statistics with positive results. But, then again, no statistics of any negative results. Remember, I am the optimist.

The doctors couldn't even offer me too many possibilities of side effects. How could they tell me side effects when no one had had it done before? I felt like I was backing myself into a corner.

Images of unexpected side effects flashed through my mind. Loss of hair, regurgitation, loss of appetite, these "normal" side effects for classic radiation may not be in Rayna's realm. But what could? Anything and everything? Nightmarish fantasies consumed my logical mind. Would her hair turn blue? Would her legs and arms shrink, would she ever be able to talk again, run again, see again, bear children? And what were the doctors' expectations? Primarily minor hair loss, only where the proton beam radiation hit it. Although, never done before, this is what they medically and scientifically anticipated. Thankfully, they were right, and in the end, my nightmares could stay buried under the pillow.

The doctors then asked me if I had any questions.

"Any questions, Sandy?"

Such a simple question. What could I ask? I definitely couldn't ask the typical questions that most patients ask when seeking reassuring answers, the ones that give them the "guaranteed assurances" that are so desperately sought when faced with difficult news. They had basically answered the ones I wanted the answers to, and my list would not look like many other lists.

"How many cases like this have been done"

"None."

"What is the success rate?"

"?"

"What are the side effects besides hair loss."

"?"

"Will she live?"

"?"

"Will she live with quality to her life?"

"?"

So, there it was, my complete list of answers. One none

and four "?" were my security blanket. I did think of one question that might come close to the security blanket I was so desperately seeking. It wouldn't give me the impossible guarantees, just one step out of the void I felt. My straws were dwindling, so I took a deep breath, looked square in the doctors' eyes and breathlessly whispered it.

"One final question. If this were your child, what would you do?"

A positive answer to this question might at least give me the encouragement to dig myself out of the sand. Unequivocally, this team felt that, although no one knows exactly how they will react until faced with a dilemma, they did indeed think that, given the circumstances, they would "go for it." Then they did one thing better than nod their heads in the affirmative. They smiled. So, I smiled. Rayna's saying was true. "If you smile at someone, someone will smile back at you."

The pros for this special radiation definitely outweighed the cons of the traditional radiation, and I certainly wasn't going to put in my vote for a seventy percent wrecking job, so with Allyn's hand in mine, we both nodded in the affirmative that we agreed with the doctor. We would try this treatment, pursue this radiation therapy, grasp onto this last straw.

This treatment had finality to it. Radiation to this area would saturate Rayna's immune system. Once an area has been radiated, the normal tissues will not tolerate any more radiation. If this was not successful in cauterizing and shrinking the blood vessels, for all intents and purposes, there was really no second chance. This was really our only hope. I didn't consider the "seventy percent wrecking Rayna" choice a choice.

A few weeks later, when all the preparations were in place, Rayna would begin proton beam radiation for her cavernous hemangioma of the thalamus and would be the first person in the world to do so. We would once again become contestants in the waiting game. I hoped our prizes would be what we wanted. Life is really such a game in so many respects.

We exited the hospital, decision made, hanging onto Rayna "for dear life," her left hand grabbing mine, Allyn's hand holding up her back, each of us armed with tissues to wipe the drool. I remembered the day, that long ago, bitter cold day, when I leaped for joy that Rayna didn't have a malignant tumor, but a blood vessel problem. I was certainly getting an education in medicine and its implications.

The outside noises seemed deafening, policemen blowing whistles, cars honking, people laughing, airplanes flying overhead. I wanted to block my ears, muffle the sounds, enter a silent world where I could prescribe its outcome, control its destiny, erase disease, poverty, homelessness, disasters. I could contribute my efforts, volunteer my time and money, but I couldn't be God. I wanted to jump inside her head, get that "thing" out of there. I knew I couldn't do that. I couldn't block my ears to the world. I couldn't do anything. My hands were busy holding up my daughter.

We came home from the doctor's appointment that day, picked Tovah up at school, helped Rayna walk up the stairs, helped her sit down in the chair. I was so emotionally spent, the only activity I could think of doing, the only thing that would keep me from these ominous feelings would be to lie down and pray for sleep to come and hope it would be free of nightmares. All Rayna wanted to do at that moment was bake.

"Mommy, I want to make brownies."

"Brownies—like you eat? Now?"

"Mommy, you're silly."

This was not the conversation I envisioned. But, then again, thank goodness for childhood and its sometimes automatic insulation. Rayna had her doctor's appointment, now she wanted to bake. I went on Rayna's doctor's appointment and now all I wanted to do was "die."

Rayna loved to bake, she loved to be in the kitchen, and she loved to be a contributing factor to the menu. The fact that she could hardly walk, had double vision, and had drool coming out of her mouth on the numbed side of her face, was not a reason in her book to give up those brownies she always loves to bake.

She loved to put on her "Mother's Little Helper" apron, have her hair pulled back, and help get out all the ingredients. Cracking the egg was one of her favorites. And I loved to watch her crack it, since she learned to do it so successfully with one hand. However, today, Tovah decided she wanted to help, too. So I backed off and let the two girls have their time together. I knew it was important for Tovah to spend some time with Rayna. She was quite frightened by all that was happening, and we were constantly giving her quiet little talks in order to keep her up with the latest details of Rayna's illness.

I am very lucky that the girls get along so well. They have a beautiful, sisterly bond. But, like most siblings, they have their "moments."

"It's my turn to mix."

"You mixed last time."

"No, sir."

"Yes, sir."

"I decided to make them so it's my turn."

"Not fair."

"Yes fair."

"Not."

"Is."

"Not."

"MOM!"

A conversation I have heard once or twice in the past, but not today. Just beautifully working together; Tovah patiently holding the bowl for Rayna so she could mix the batter. Things were fine until Rayna drooled.

"Yuck, that's disgusting," Tovah proclaimed.

I explained to Tovah it wasn't Rayna's fault, that she didn't feel it, as I gently wiped her face while my heart crumbled in a million pieces. The phone rang and I went into the other room to talk. Entering the kitchen again, I noticed that Rayna had drooled some more. Before I had a chance to pick up a Kleenex, Tovah very matter-of-factly took a Kleenex out of the box, walked over to her sister and gently wiped her face, then just as matter-of-factly, resumed baking. I had to leave the room again. I didn't want my tears to spoil their fun. I was so proud of Tovah. There was so much love in her eyes as she gently wiped her sister's face, so wise beyond her years, so giving.

Since the day Rayna was diagnosed, Allyn and I have always been very careful not to leave Tovah out, not to abandon this child for the other. Rayna had different needs from her sister; these did not erase Tovah's needs. Both children need us as parents, just in varied ways. We always tried to have "alone time" with each girl, and never to minimize Tovah's needs. Running out of kindergarten with her drawings, recounting a story of how Miss Metcalf picked her to be the weather girl for the day, and how she and Emily and Chantal were the first to see the baby chicks hatch, always took precedence over any news I would deliver. We'd walk out of school together, Tovah's daily activities spilling out of her. She'd hold her papers in one hand and clutch my hand with her other.

Yes, spending time with each girl was special, always was and always will be.

I remember when Rayna was first able to sit in the car on the seat instead of a car seat. Every time we would go somewhere, the girls would climb in the back and I would automatically turn to Tovah.

"Please buckle your sister."

Tovah would oblige without saying a word. One day, several months later, I asked, as always for Tovah to buckle Rayna and she emphatically announced that she doesn't always want to buckle her sister and please don't ask her anymore. So I didn't. I decided this six-year-old had enough demands being made upon her as the sibling of a child with special needs, I wasn't going to add seat belt buckling to it.

The next time we were all going out together, I quickly seat belted Rayna before I got into the driver's side. Soon after that, we were going to school, and I needed to run back in the house before I had a chance to buckle Rayna. When I returned to the garage to the driver's seat, I realized I hadn't buckled Rayna yet, but when I got out to do so, she was already buckled and Tovah was sitting there smiling sweetly at me. I felt such pride. She really did want to help her sister, help take care of her. How did I deserve to have such a wonderful daughter?

Any upset in the harmony of the family affects everyone, and Tovah has certainly had her share. Through it all, she has been a wonderful sister to Rayna, so compassionate and understanding. Yes, two wonderful daughters.

Word got out very quickly about the devastation that once again had plagued our family. This crippling bleed had happened on the weekend, just prior to Rosh Hashanah, the Jewish New Year. Rayna was looking forward to worshipping in temple as she does every year. Another disappointment in life, she would be spending the holiday in the hospital.

Early in the morning, the day before the holiday, the doorbell rang. Standing there was the rabbi. Rayna's face lit up with excitement and zest, for her adoration for this man was immense. He had just been given the news about Rayna and had found his way to our house within minutes. He stood for a few minutes talking to her. I never noticed that he kept one hand behind his back the whole time.

"You know, Rayna, I was very sorry to hear you won't be in temple tomorrow."

And Rayna nodded her head sadly.

"You know, Rayna, I know how much you love to hear the Shofar being blown."

And Rayna nodded her head sadly.

"You know, Rayna," the rabbi said as he pulled out a shofar (a ram's horn musical instrument used since ancient times in Jewish religious ceremonies) from behind his back, "I should like to blow the shofar for you now."

And Rayna smiled as big a smile as her numbed face would allow.

The rabbi took her into the den, sat her down, and blew the shofar for her. For her, his private audience. For her, someone he truly adored and compassionately suffered for as much as we did. The melodic sound permeated the quiet of this Sunday morning, and I stood listening with such admiration for this man, for the deep-rooted love he was bestowing on my daughter, for the gift of love he was presenting to Rayna and to us as well.

Slowly, but very slowly, Rayna began once again to have her "spontaneous recovery" from this third bleed. The double vision slowly dissipated, and her walk gradually got stronger. Her drooling took a little longer to subside. We felt it would be best for her to sleep in our bed. She felt safer if she could sleep next to one of us, to have someone right next to her to hold her up as she walked to the bathroom if she awoke in the middle of the night and needed to do so. I opted to sleep in her bed, while she had the security of Allyn next to her.

Staying in Rayna's room was cozy. I felt like a little girl again, all safe and snuggled in her little bed, with all the make believe world of stuffed animals and beautiful dolls with golden curls. I'd cuddle under the covers, her beautiful coordinated sheets, precious little flowers of violets, pinks and yellows. I'd try to work on my latest script, or read some escapist novel, not really interested at this point in either, just looking for something to put me to sleep. For eight hours a night, I left all the turmoil of being the mother of a sick child, became the little girl I had long left behind, then at seven A.M., I would face the morning and reality and walk into my bedroom as the mother waking up her daughter. But, the next night, I would once again return to that dream world of childhood.

We had to meet several times with the radiation therapy doctor prior to the beginning of the radiation. The first step was to place pins in Rayna's head; they would be the target points to locate the areas for radiation. Next, a localizing mask had to be made, as well as preradiation clinical exams to be conducted. Although the radiation was to take place at the Cyclotron in Cambridge, Massachusetts, these appointments were conducted at the radiotherapy department of the Massachusetts General Hospital. The radiation department is located in the basement, something to do with shielding for the machines, but how depressing it was to press the down button on the elevator. Aren't our lives down enough?

The first time we went to meet with the doctor, we checked in and sat down in a rather large waiting area. I looked around at the various people there, some were balding, some wore kerchiefs, but, somehow I sensed exactly what their latest hairdo looked like underneath those kerchiefs. I looked around at all these people in the course of their radiation treatments, mainly for malignancies.

The first thought that came to my mind in reacting to this atmosphere was a comment I remembered overhearing more than thirteen years ago. Allyn and I had gone on a chartered trip to Jamaica. The same plane that was to take us home was the same one that brought the new arrivals for the next week. Those were the days when we weren't as knowledgeable of the negative effects of suntanning and the same one hundred and ten travelers who had descended the plane with pale faces only a week earlier were now returning home as brown as could be. As the new arrivals came off the plane for their week of vacation, a very tanned woman, standing next to me, laughed out loud and turned to her friend, equally as tanned.

"Here come the new arrivals. Ship them down, brown them up, ship them home." And she laughed.

I looked around at these victims of disease, each getting radiation, and that was all I could think of. Ship in the patients, "radiate" them up and ship them out (hopefully cured). It's amazing how the mind works. Oh well, a little humor helps alleviate the fears, at least for a second. How could I laugh at a time like this?

Then I thought about something my cousin Barbara had said. Her mother, my aunt, had just been diagnosed with Alzheimer's Disease. My cousin was doing her best to cope with it, but was quite distraught over the diagnosis. She decided to join a support group for families of Alzheimer victims. On the first night of the meeting, while my cousin was looking for the room, nervous about the whole situation, another woman approached her asking if she knew where to find the room for the meeting of the Alzheimer support group. My cousin looked at her and very seriously said, "Yes, but I forget," then broke out laughing. Unfortunately the woman did not see the humor. In relating this story to me, she insisted that you need humor, that it helps alleviate the tension, the fears, the stress. Perhaps that woman should read Norman Cousins.

My cousin is right. You need humor. Everyone does—the patient and those dealing with the patient. I remembered one night a few weeks prior to the proposed stereotactic biopsy; remembering as the days got closer to the surgery, my fears got bigger. One night, Allyn made a comment that reminded me of a funny event that happened to us many years earlier. We started reliving it and laughing about it.

I reminded him of the time, one autumn, when he was in his residency and one of the nurses asked us if we would volunteer some time for a group in which she was quite active. It was a group of inner-city, less fortunate boys and girls that she would spend Saturdays with at some country retreat. Since Allyn and I were both actively doing a lot of photography at that time, she asked us if we would put together some type of photography program. We talked it over and decided we would first show them slides of our work. We would then take a nature walk giving them some suggestions of how to take pictures. We decided to donate some Polaroid film so each child could take a picture and have a souvenir of the day. Perfect. Well, almost perfect.

I had picked my tray of slides filled with wonderful autumn scenes and lighthouses, my specialty. Allyn got called out on an emergency the night before and didn't have a chance to select his pictures until that morning. Quite fatigued from the night before, yet not wanting to cancel out on this commitment, he grabbed what he thought were his slides of the winter scenes in Vermont. We put my slides on first and everything was going quite nicely until he popped his tray of slides in.

When the first picture appeared, it showed me standing in our apartment in front of our stereo system and I suspected something was wrong. When the next slide showed a close up of my diamond engagement ring, I knew something was definitely wrong. It took Allyn a few more slides to realize that he had accidentally picked the tray of slides documenting our valuables for insurance purposes. These were clearly not Vermont in winter, but embarrassment in autumn. Somehow, I don't think this is what inner-city, low income children wanted to see. In reminiscing, we started laughing loudly at the ludicrous scene that this had made. Tears were coming to our eyes we were laughing so hard. Ah, yes, for a few brief moments, we escaped the heavy feeling and felt some comic relief.

"Hey, quiet you guys," the girls screamed at us. Better they should be mad that they couldn't hear the television from us laughing so loud than from arguing with each other. They had enough to deal with.

Next, I tried to list in my mind all the cute expressions the girls said as children, and how each time these words had made me smile. Tovah's early name for Rayna was Nina, and Rayna in turn declared her sister's name to be "Ovah." "Baboon" substituted for ice cream cone, "kakoo" for airplane, "dosies" for horse. Come on, Sandy, think of some more, don't let that smile fade, you can do it. Oh, yeah, Tovah's declaration of arriving home after an outing was "e e ah," later to be interpreted by my mother as "Here we are."

Okay, I'm on a roll. This is good. Think of more. Don't look at that lady starting to wretch and the nurse helping her out of the room; don't look at that teenager with a kerchief on her head. Oh, good, I have another one.

One time, Tovah was lying on the living-room rug attempting to draw a picture on a piece of paper and kept punching through the paper with her pencil. I suggested she lean on a magazine to give her support. She thanked me for the idea, then leaned over to the magazine rack, extracted a large magazine and slid it under her stomach. I guess if I'm going to be a successful writer, I may need to communicate my ideas just a little bit better!

So, I sat in that waiting room trying to conjure up some comic relief. I figured if I could start shaking from laughing, it would cover up my shaking from fright. I looked around at the radiation patients, searching for the next ludicrous thought. Whatever problem Rayna has, I thought, thank God it isn't cancer. As soon as the thought was formulated, I questioned it. How could I even think that? Why would I thank God it wasn't cancer? There have been many cancer victims cured. My daughter is walking around with a time bomb in her head and I'm still thankful it isn't cancer. I was still trying to figure out how I put a walking time bomb in a ten-year-old's head a step ahead of cancer when her name was called. Good thing I hadn't given up the psychologist.

The doctor did an extensive examination on everything, carefully documenting each move, each answer. It was then time to have an immobilizing mask made. This entailed Rayna lying still on a table while they made a plastic mold of her face, then hardened it. She would be wearing this facsimile to a goalie's mask for all her treatments. This would be a necessity for precise targeting of the radiation.

In three weeks her radiation treatments would start. In three weeks, Rayna would start on a venture that hopefully would have a happy ending. She would either be the first successful patient or a failed test case. The radiation would either cauterize these blood vessels so they would never bleed again or it wouldn't.

In three weeks she would try a new path down this road. Maybe this one would finally lead to that pot of gold. That gave me hope.

In three weeks she would be the first recipient of this radiation. That gave me hope—and fear.

No-choice choices.

Chapter Seven

ONE DAY IN HER LIFE

On October 24, 1991, at the age of ten, Rayna's radiation began. Medical history was going to be made. This was the first test case of twenty-five fractionated proton beam radiation for a cavernous hemangioma in the thalamus. The result could be either success or failure. My daughter was going to be cured or not.

I tried to put it into perspective. I tried to play the "It could always be worse game," and this time it really helped a lot. After all, people came from all over the world to have this treatment, since there are only a few machines like it in the world. They uprooted their lives, traveling thousands of miles, sleeping in prearranged living places, perhaps uprooting siblings, or worrying about them left home with other caretakers.

All we had was a twenty-five minute ride from Newton, and we got to go home at night to the security of our home and family. Besides these inconveniences, most of the kinds of problems that patients are treated for by this radiation require two treatments a day, one in the morning and one later in the day. Rayna's condition only warranted one treatment a day. At least we didn't have to go twice. Also, this particular type of radiation had minimal side effects. I guess there is a rainbow at the end of the storm, some good to look for in the bad. Putting it in perspective is like throwing cold water on your face. I guess I was becoming an expert at this.

I was intrigued and overwhelmed at the same time by the statistics concerning this machine. With only a few existing in the world, they were originally designed as research tools for physicists. The construction of the machine started in 1945. They are, in reality, "atom smashers," which cause collisions between nuclear particles which then emit radiation. About twenty-five years ago, they began using them on human beings for certain brain tumors. The first proton beam was given in June of 1949 (the month and year I was born). The cost was 1.5 million dollars. The weight of the steel is six hundred forty-one tons. Mind-boggling statistics, mind-boggling applications, a human, a man, a woman, a child—my child.

I reviewed the facts. Rayna, in actuality, was a "guinea pig" for three firsts with this machine. It had never been used on anyone in the world with her condition (cavernous hemangioma in the left thalamus); it had never been given in fractionated (divided over weeks) dosages for this type of tumor; they had never used this treatment without some conventional radiation therapy to augment it. The fact that a hard scientific research instrument was used as a therapeutic instrument was miraculous in itself. I knew that my daughter would be written up in medical journals. I only hoped it would be written as a success story.

We talked with the school of the possibility of home tutoring, but opted for a two hour school day instead. Rayna really wanted to be in school, and everyone involved thought the socialization would be helpful. She would go to school until eleven o'clock, come home, have lunch and rest, then go to the Cyclotron.

We quickly settled into a routine. It's truly amazing how we always seek that out in the midst of chaos. We hang onto some kind of routine, because that gives us security, reassurance, and safety. It gives us a sense of security to have ritual, to have sameness and familiarity. Rituals and kids, in my book, are synonymous. Rayna has developed many rituals over the years; the most prevalent is when she gets her hormone shots. No matter how tired, how late, how distracted she may be at the time, she has her set of questions before she will allow either of us to give her the shot.

"What side is it going on?"

"Is it too much?"

"Where's it going to go?" And we have to press on the spot with the alcohol pad.

These questions, routinely asked every night prior to the shot, are what give Rayna her protection from the pain of the shot. I'm not really sure it's the answers she is seeking, but rather the need to ask the questions. And it's like music to my ears, for I know these questions are her comfort, her barrier, her private world.

I would drop Rayna off at school and spend a good part of the next two hours exercising. That would give me a sense of peace, as much peace I could have these days.

So, life settled into this routine. We'd drive to the Cyclotron, perhaps be taken right away or have to wait a little if the treatment before Rayna ran late. Rayna, being the friendly person that she is, the magnetic personality, would love to greet everyone. Even Sal, the custodian, became a special friend to Rayna, each looking forward to one another's bright smiles and warm hellos.

Rayna would have to climb onto a large table and have the localizing mask placed over her head, secured down with what looked like a tennis racket holder. The mask was a most uncomfortable apparatus for anyone, let alone a ten-year-old, to be confined in for twenty minutes to an hour. This would absolutely insure that Rayna's head could not move and the therapists could position the radiation more precisely. Most of the time was for setup with only eighty seconds for the actual radiation. Several x-rays would have to be taken, then charted out, then they had to reposition Rayna, and so on and so on until the last five minutes.

I'd stand right next to her the whole time except when we would all have to leave while the x-rays were being taken, and of course, during the actual treatment. Some days I would read her a story. The book we chose to read was *The Secret Garden*. Looking back, I wonder if this was a subconscious selection. Did we view these daily jaunts to Cambridge as our secret haven where the world was going to be bright and wonderful in the end? Some days I would go over her spelling words with her for the next day's test. Since Rayna could not move, or speak, I would say the words out loud and spell them for her. If I needed to ask her a question, one blink was a yes, two blinks a no, our little invention for a means of communicating.

Some days she didn't feel like doing anything, just lie there, secure in the fact that I was right next to her, giving her all the protection I could in this environment. Once in a while, she would fall asleep, and that would be my favorite time, because time wouldn't be so prevalent on her mind, and she would not have to make such an effort to lie there and be patient. Her mind could be passively relaxed, and she could escape into a wonderful dream world. I would watch her, eyes closed, and watch the technicians busy with their calculations. These were calculations that I didn't know whether to be in awe of or in fear of. Modern technology is something that has always amazed, yet frightened me. It is also something that has saved my daughter's life. I guess awe wins out over fright.

I would shift my eyes from Rayna's closed ones to reading the same signs over and over again. I really studied the formation in the letters of the EXIT sign, the words KEEP OUT, and some days I would just stare at the different shoes the technicians wore, wondering which were more comfortable. One technician wore the greatest slacks; the hem always hit her shoes in just the right place. She also won my award for the best jewelry.

On a good day, when all the calculations went well, we'd be out of there in twenty to twenty-five minutes; on a bad day—one hour.

When everything was all set, when the fields were lined up exactly, when her head was in the exact position, when they were almost ready to "return" my daughter to me, they would call into an intercom to the main control area and say "five minute warning." This meant that they needed the doctor to come in and check all the calculations and the final place where the radiation would travel that day. They would start recording their findings and the doctor would enter to check it all. If the doctor gave the thumbs up, we'd all leave (my euphemism for abandon) Rayna and walk out of the room. A large ominous door would shut behind us with authority, bolted, so that no accidental entry was made during this time. The technicians, the doctor, and I would go into the control room. I'd sit there watching numerous control switches being flipped on, the technician matching numbers written by the radiotherapists to those on his control panel, and then it would begin. "It"—the cure? the hero? the demon? the Almighty Savior? the good guy? the bad guy? the rescuer of this nightmare? I would know it was happening, because as the radiation went into Rayna's head, it would make a sound. On the days Allyn was able to take Rayna, he would know it was happening by following the path of energy on an oscilloscope. Funny, separated by a few feet down a hallway, I couldn't be with Rayna for those eighty seconds, but that sound bonded me to Rayna, for my heart would skip a beat and I would cringe inside as I listened to the noise. As soon as it was over, we quickly returned to Rayna, unbolted the door, unscrewed the head mask, took off the lead apron, and helped her off the table. I would be so happy it was over, at least for another day.

We had a little game, starting from the very first day. One down, twenty-four to go, two down, twenty-three to go. I prayed for the day that we said twenty-five down, zero to go.

The mask would come off, and underneath would be Rayna, all smiles, cheerful good-byes, see-you-tomorrows. I wish I had her beautiful soul and could be the kind of person who would be caught in a burning building and ask the fireman how his wife and kids are! That's Rayna—always concerned for the other, always more interested in the welfare of the other person. Someone once came to see Rayna in the hospital, walked in the room as she lay on the hospital bed and as soon as they entered the room, Rayna's face brightened.

When she asked, "So, how are you?" the person looked startled and taken aback.

"How am I?" she asked incredulously. "Ah, fine, I guess. I thought I was the one to ask you that."

That's my Rayna. One Thanksgiving she wanted to take all her allowance, every penny, and give it to the homeless. One holiday season, her Girl Scout troop had a gift swap. Rayna picked in the bag, opened her gift, a cute pencil set that she adored. It was soon realized that one child forgot to bring a gift so was unable to select one. Within minutes the pencil set was in that girl's hands. "Better to give than to receive." Rayna knew nor felt no other alternative.

I can sum all these praises up with one final story. If Rayna had five cents left to her name and was asked by someone for ten cents, she would not only give up her five cents, but also find the other five cents.

And, if I may brag, these attributes didn't end at Rayna. I remember the first time I allowed Tovah to go to a mall alone with a friend. With her spending money tucked securely away, she ventured out to a new freedom, spending her money alone, away from me. She returned, excited with her new found adventure, her new grown-up activity, and her purchases. Included among these were a gift for her mother, her father, and her sister.

I admire my children's values.

It's amazing how you can spend relatively little time with some people, yet it can seem like a lifetime. From October 24,

1991 to December 6, 1991, for twenty-five almost consecutive days, Rayna spent time at the Cyclotron, looking for the cure, hoping for the miracle, trying to find the needle in the haystack, hoping to be the first success story of this radiation—a miracle and not a guinea pig. For most of the treatments I was her escort; on a few Allyn was able to get away from work. Her average treatment lasted from twenty minutes to an hour. I thought about this and realized that when she finished her treatments, she had basically spent only enough hours to make up the equivalent of a day, approximately twenty-four hours, one day out of many in a year, in a lifetime. One day. How much do we do in one day, in twenty-four hours? Yet, these people became an integral part of our lives. They became like second families to us. We knew about them, their education, their personal lives, if outsiders, why they chose Boston, why they chose radiation for careers, and why proton beam radiation. Even the secretary and the custodian became our friends. Yet, this whole experience was only comparable to one day.

Hearing the words "five minute warning" became music to my ears. They were the happiest words of the day. The day I said "twenty-five down, zero to go" was the ultimate symphony.

Saying good-bye that last day was no easy task. We arrived with our arms filled with gifts, a huge fruit basket for all to share. A partylike atmosphere prevailed as Rayna descended the radiation table for the last time, took off the mask for the last time, the last time I heard that five minute warning, the last time I would stand by my daughter staring at her vulnerable body as she gave herself over to technicians, technology, and God.

"You take care of yourself, Rayna."

"Come back and visit."

"We're glad you're done."

We hugged, we cried, and we cheered. We took pictures. Pictures for souvenirs, for memories, for never forgetting, for a reminder, for always—as if I didn't have it implanted in my memory forever. With promises to return and visit as "civilians," we turned our backs and for the final time walked out of the Cyclotron. For no matter what resulted, what the treatments did for her, this was as far as this technology could go.

Driving home that last night, it seemed only fitting that it was raining. I don't know why it felt fitting, it just did. Maybe because a rainbow sometimes appears after the rain, and at the rainbow is a pot of gold, and I believed our pot of gold was going to come in the form of a successful result from this treatment.

And so we finished, and since it takes approximately six months for any kind of results to show up on an MRI, I had six months to wait, to pray, and to hope.

Ironically, Rayna's radiation finished on December 6, 1991, and we went out to celebrate. December sixth, a day to rejoice, a day to celebrate the end, and hopefully the beginning. The end of ill health, the beginning of new found health. An important day to always remember, but then again, it's a day I had never forgotten. It was the day my mother had died eight years earlier. Yes, I guess it was a celebration, for my mother would have been there on this day, smiling with pride at her granddaughter, and praying just as hard as all of us that this treatment be successful. Boy, did I miss my parents.

Toward the last five treatments, the inevitable happened, something the doctors had warned me would probably happen. Where the proton beam was targeted, hair loss began and would continue for a few weeks after. Rayna was soon left with a huge bald spot on the top of her head. Since she wasn't into hats, try as we could, we had difficulty in trying to cover it up. The only successful thing we found was a wide head band, which Rayna found, in the end, uncomfortable, and so she chose blatant baldness over uncomfortable disguise. In other words, she used logic over vanity, she'd rather be comfortable than hide her baldness with something that made her feel uncomfortable. I guess this isn't surprising from someone who had been through numerous IVs, CAT scans,

MRIs, blood tests, and a host of other uncomfortable situations. She wasn't about to add uncomfortable headbands to her list.

The bald spot became a symbol to me, a message, a reminder, an announcement to the world. I would look at it and cringe, feel sorry for what Rayna had to endure. I'd look at and beam with pride at what she had to endure and how heroic she was. I'd look at it and be angry for what she had to endure, and I'd look at it and be grateful that this might have helped her. I'd look at it and be intrigued at what can happen to the human body. I'd look at it and be scared at what can happen to the human body. I'd look at it and be hopeful that in six months I'd have an answer. I'd look at it and dread the answer to come would be, once again, one I didn't want to hear.

After all those weeks, those drives, those endless hours between treatments, it felt a lot longer than one day in her life.

Chapter Eight

AND LIFE GOES ON—AGAIN

Our new found routine of short school days and hot lunches in front of silly sitcoms was about to come to an end. An adjustment period from December sixth to the holiday break was put into Rayna's schedule, in hope of returning to school full-time in January. So, little by little, we were going to have to skip knowing what was behind door number three that day, or if Cindi and Marsha solved their argument with Greg and Peter, or if Jeannie got back her magical powers. It's amazing how much passivity the mind can absorb, how dependent we can become on the television for our fantasy time, our escape time.

Rayna mustered up her strength and attempted to increase her school day. She really wanted to be back in school like all the other kids, like all the other teachers, like all the other normal people.

And me? I had to readjust to the real world, the world she should have been in all along, of laughing with friends and spending carefree weekends going to the movies instead of spending days in a mask that made her sweaty with her only form of communication a blink.

I would walk into a supermarket with the whole experience still weighing heavily on my mind. At the checkout counter, I would be so absorbed in my thoughts that when I was asked, paper or plastic, I would resent such a difficult decision.

Then I would wonder when I was supposed to stop answering every question or justifying every action with "my daughter just finished radiation." If someone would cut me off while driving, I would get angry and think how dare he cut me off, my daughter just finished radiation. Doesn't he know what I'm going through? Everything I did and thought during the radiation period and after was based on that single thought. I didn't know when I was supposed to let go of it. How long was "just" finished? How long could I continue to think about it day and night and feel betrayed by a careless driver for cutting me off when my daughter "just" finished radiation? How long was "just"—a few weeks after, a few months, a year, a lifetime? I needed to put this behind me, yet I needed never to forget. Finding that harmonious balance is not something I had ever learned in birth class.

As the weeks passed, and Rayna's hair grew back, and the world no longer saw the physical signs of Rayna's ordeal, the days at the Cyclotron didn't have a front seat in my mind, just a permanent back seat.

It was time to move Rayna back into her own room, to return to "normalcy." Fear set in. Rayna still did not have the confidence to sleep in her room by herself, so we decided to purchase an intercom system so that if Rayna needed us, she could just talk into the intercom.

I knew baby stores would have these, so that's the first

place I stopped to look for one. Sure enough, there were several varieties from which to choose. I engaged the help of a sales girl, only expressing a need for one, not disclosing my reason. I was doing fine until she asked me a question.

"How old is the baby?"

Ten, and she'll always be my baby.

"Ah, it's not for a baby, it's for...well, it's a long story...I'll just take this one." I paid as quickly as I could and left before I said what I really wanted to say.

I think the truest challenge of "just" finished radiation came about five months after the cessation of the treatments. I knew that Rayna was going to have obstacles in her life, some I planned on, most I never even dreamed of. I think everyone, with or without special needs, encounters obstacles. We all have to face them, meet them head on, learn how to deal with them, attempt to overcome them, and then move on. One of the things I try to teach Rayna, as well as Tovah, is how to fight their own battles. I would step in and assist to teach them how to do this. It could be as simple as how to share a toy or decide who gets which program on the television. I believe in trying to teach the girls how to fight their own battles, how to meet their own challenges, and then there are the battles that I go to bat for, in this case, almost to war for. At least it was our own private war.

Rayna was looking forward to the area games of the Special Olympics as she had the year before, her first year as a member. She had enjoyed these local games the previous year as well as the state Olympics. Now, as a second year member, she eagerly looked forward to competing in her sport, tennis. Tennis was something the orthopedic surgeon had suggested Rayna get involved with, because it would accomodate her weaknesses and be helpful for her. He was more than right. From the moment Rayna joined up with the dozen or so handicapped members of the team, she thrived. She felt so at home with this group of special needs children. Rayna has always fallen "between the cracks" with her disability. She isn't quite able to keep up with a regular sports team or dance class, yet doesn't quite belong with physically impaired groups either. Her handicap with her right-sided weakness is just impeding enough, yet not quite severe enough to seem to fit into too many defined groups—like a swinging pendulum.

In comparison to the various problems of these children, Rayna was the "least handicapped," the brightest, and all around, I guess you'd say, the luckiest. Yet, she has never questioned why she was with a group less "normal" than she, but, rather, eagerly awaited Saturdays every week when she could be with her tennis buddies, her other classmates, her friends. She'd hug them hello, hug them good-bye, and in between enjoy an hour with children with mental retardation, Down's syndrome, and assorted other problems. In essence, she felt at home, no challenges, no huffing and puffing to keep up with the "norm," as well as an enormous appreciation and understanding of how lucky she was to be as well off as she was with her condition. No frustrations, only satisfaction.

She, as well as I, also loved her coach, a wonderful mother and teacher whose own daughter, one with many problems, is part of the team. As the day approached that May for the area games, ominous weather forecasts predicted rain—raw, windy, and generally a nasty day. We had a number to call that day where we would be told if the games were to be held or postponed a week. Rayna went to bed that night with much excitement for the day and much anxiety over the weather. At six-thirty the next morning she appeared at my bedside holding the paper with the phone number. As I dialed the number, she looked out at the bleak weather. A recording came on the phone telling me that since the weather forecasts announced clearing up later in the day, they were going to go ahead and try to hold the area games.

I hung up the phone, sat with Rayna, and discussed the situation. In ten days, we were having a major family function with many out-of-town guests and friends. It was wet and raw out and the games were being played forty-five minutes away. We were both fearful of Rayna getting sick, and, with much courage, Rayna made a very grown-up decision not to play the area games. I had even tried to help her some more in making that decision by reassuring her that she still had the wonderful weekend of the state games where people from all over the state come together to compete. I knew what a difficult decision it was for her to make, and I was very proud of her.

The following week when we went to tennis, the coach asked what happened to us the week before, and we explained that the weather was so bad, Rayna was afraid of being on the wet ground and out in the rain, and we had decided to forego it this time, but we would be at the state games. The coach then informed me that because Rayna didn't compete in the area games, a forerunner to the state games, she was now ineligible to play in the state games. I couldn't believe what she was telling me and told her that she had never made us aware of any such rule. She apologized for this misunderstanding and gave me the number of the Special Olympics state office. I figured a two minute phone call Monday morning would straighten this out right away. I was never so wrong.

First thing Monday morning, I called, told our story, and was politely informed that rules are rules and that indeed Rayna could not play in the state games. I couldn't believe what I was hearing. Nothing I said would convince them. Yes, they were very sorry about my misinformation, but there was nothing they could do this year and there was always next year.

My daughter has a bleeding lesion in her head that experimental radiation may or may not have cured. I don't think she is going to wait another three hundred and sixty-five days to compete in the state games.

"Please tell me who else I can talk to."

I was given the number of the next higher authority, given the same incredible news, that, although it was a mistake, sorry, but it wouldn't be fair to those who didn't qualify in the area games. I defended that one with the information that the coach had given me; there weren't enough entries in the tennis matches to eliminate anyone. Everyone qualified. So, Rayna wouldn't be jumping ahead of someone who hadn't qualified. Next argument? This went on and on, until I got to the highest authority. No, not God, but the executive director. He merely summed up all the arguments and that was that. Maybe "that was that" for them, but not for me or Rayna. We hadn't traveled this far in the journey of life for some head of an organization to tell me "sorry, next year"—not for me, not for Rayna. I wrote a letter, a beautiful letter pouring my heart out, rehashing all that had been said, but to no avail. I went so far as to call my lawyer and ask him for advice.

As I was driving to the lawyer's office to discuss the situation with him, something occurred to me, and I later had an intense discussion with both girls. I explained to them that I was fighting for this cause because I believed an injustice had been done, a wrong needed to be righted. It, in its essence, had absolutely nothing to do with the fact that Rayna had special needs, and that if I felt some injustice had been done to Tovah, I would want that corrected as well. This wasn't about special needs, but about life's rules and unfairness. We can't always have everything the way we want, but we can certainly fight for the causes we believe in. Some fights are "worth" it, and some aren't. This was "worth" it. Some fights they would need to fight themselves, and some I would fight. And this was one of them. Another life lesson.

What finally occurred after ten days of phone calls, letters, and another round of sleepless nights, was the ruling that if a participant had a doctor's letter explaining why the child couldn't participate in the area games, that would be accepted and participation in the state games would be allowed. I called Rayna's neurologist and explained the situation. Of course, our decision not to play that rainy day was warranted. After all, as we both reviewed, the immediate side effects from the radiation could lower her immune system and make her more susceptible to infection. Within the hour, I drove to the hospital, picked up the letter, faxed it to the headquarters, and received the news I should have received ten days ago—that Rayna could now participate in the state games. An official letter followed this decision with an apology for all the trouble that had been caused. Despite this altercation, I still truly support the Special Olympics and its wonderful efforts, forgiving this oversight. The bottom line was that Rayna was going to have a weekend of good sportsmanship and mega doses of self-esteem. So she played, and she won a gold medal. And she told me this was one of her happiest days, not because she won a medal, but because she was trying her best, cheering on her team, and being with special people who cared.

I sat there with all the other families at the opening ceremonies, watching with endless pride as more than two thousand athletes walked or "wheeled" onto the field amidst cheering, yelling, and clapping. It was the truest of lessons in putting things in their proper place, of really being thankful for what you have.

No matter what the infirmity, every parent there had the same common bond. We all got the unexpected, we all delivered children we didn't plan on, picked out names, decorated the nursery. We've all spent endless hours in doctors' offices, hospitals; we've all shed buckets of tears, had sleepless nights; we've all had our hearts broken.

And life goes on—again.

Chapter Nine

THE HURRICANE WAS OVER

Since it takes approximately six months for anything to show up on an MRI, I had at least until June 6 to find out if my prayers were answered. And since we make a yearly trip to Duke University in September and have Rayna's MRI there, the neuroradiologist felt it best to wait until then for the MRI—in fact it would give even a greater chance of hopefully seeing some kind of change. So, now what? I had approximately three more months to wait it out, nine altogether. The last time I had nine months to wait something out was…

Nine months to hope that Rayna's lesion shrunk, was cauterized, was stopped, to prevent doing any more harm to her, to ending this nightmare. Nine months, approximately thirty-six weeks, about 252 days.

The summer came with all its hazy, lazy days, and the girls

thrived in their summer activities. The shelf housing winter hats and mittens now displayed bright towels and sunscreen. I spent my days writing, exercising, and doing all the domestic necessities to keep the household running. As September drew near, and the days got shorter, the temperatures not quite so high, and the summer wound down, I found myself getting very edgy and irritable. As much as I looked forward to the trip to Duke to finally learn the outcome of the radiation, I dreaded the possibility that it wasn't successful. For there was nowhere left to turn. The road didn't go any further. Everything that could be done to abate this lesion had been done, other than taking that seventy percent chance to "wreck" Rayna. I found myself very anxious.

A few weeks prior to the trip, I received a very exciting phone call from a producer. They wanted an option on a script of mine for a movie of the week. I was overjoyed that I had my first piece of success. Yet this joy was masked by the upcoming trip. Friends who heard of this writing accomplishment congratulated me. But, I couldn't get truly excited or truly accept congratulations until Rayna got a successful answer. I couldn't truly celebrate my success unless Rayna had a success.

As the trip neared, I dug deep down again for the courage that had sustained me since all this began, almost nine years ago. We were due to be in Duke the day after Labor Day, then return to have the girls start school. They would each be in school only a day or two before leaving for a trip to Hawaii. Allyn was lecturing at an oral surgery convention, and we all were taking this opportunity to travel with him and share a wonderful vacation in Hawaii. The timing was quite interesting. Five days after our trip to Duke we were going to paradise. Or was paradise really going to be found in the confines of a room that housed an MRI machine?

The trip down to North Carolina proved uneventful in itself with the routine clinical examination and the MRI. We truly admire this doctor and feel strongly about keeping up our yearly visits to him. As in previous years, because of the fact that we are so far away and only spend one day there, Dr. DeLong has to read over all the calculations and results of the MRI and telephone us at home a few days later. He assured us he would call by Friday since we were leaving for Hawaii on Saturday.

The plane trip home brought mixed emotions of relief that clinically he felt she was doing fine, but this still didn't prove whether or not the radiation worked in cauterizing and stopping these blood vessels from doing any more harm. Only the MRI would prove this. I remembered a plane ride across the country a little over a year ago; it seemed like a lifetime ago, sitting on that plane, Rayna next to me, her right hand hanging limp, oblivious to the impending doom about to be set upon her. Yes, we had come a long way in only fourteen months, but I wanted it to be over.

On the Friday after our return, I divided up my time in three ways. I packed for paradise, stared at the phone, and listened to the weather reports of the impending Hurricane Iniki that was due to hit the islands of Hawaii sometime that night, perhaps making it impossible for us to carry out this trip. (We were going to Oahu only, so if it didn't hit there, we could still go.)

All those plans for months for this exciting trip might be canceled. I guess it wasn't the first time that things didn't turn out in life the way I had planned. "The best laid plans of mice and men often go awry,"—one of my father's favorite expressions. I carry that expression with me always.

On the Friday after our return, late in the day, three things happened. I finished packing. We listened to some more weather reports. Dr. DeLong called.

Dr. DeLong informed us that the radiation had indeed cauterized the blood vessels, even shrunk the mass it left when it had bled.

WE WON THE BATTLE.

In one little phone call, a few measured words, our world had changed once again.

As Rayna and I danced in the kitchen, hugging each other

and crying with joy, I shouted for Tovah and Allyn. They ran into the room. I stood there with the two best girls in the world, my two best friends, as Tovah announced she had just heard on the news that the hurricane was over.

Yes, the hurricane was over.

Chapter Ten

"THE WIND BENEATH MY WINGS"

Rayna was the first person in the entire world to have twenty-five fractionated treatments of proton beam radiation for a cavernous hemangioma of the left thalamus. I was wrong when I said earlier that the discovery made so long ago during that famous weekend was one that was not going to change the world, just our world. Medicine now had one more feather in its cap, one more success story, one more battle won against disease. When medical personnel, journals, and books refer to a "ten-year-old female," the usual words assigned to the patient, they're talking about Rayna, my Rayna, my ten-year-old, mine. When I gave birth to Rayna, I had dreamed about all the wonderful new things that would happen to her in life, all the "firsts"—first steps, first words, first sentences, first day at school, first boyfriend, first dance, first kiss, first child…Never did that list include this first medical breakthrough.

Rayna still faces many challenges, many hurdles, but at least one hurdle has passed. She has always faced these challenges, and there is no doubt in my mind that she will always continue to do so.

The person who had said so long ago that Rayna's problem was God's way of testing me, that He was knocking, really summed it all up.

I know now that I have the courage and stamina to withstand life's challenges, that if I hear a "knock," I will answer it with as much courage as Rayna has always done.

She truly is the wind beneath my wings.

Epilogue

As of this moment, as this book is being published, Rayna continues to improve daily, strengthening her arm, leg, and spirit. The drooling still occurs occasionally. Her MRIs, showing continued shrinking, give us only positive, happy news. Her lesion is half its original size.

She knows that this is all behind her; life looks long and good to her. She has always had a zest for life. It just got zestier.

She continues to get a nightly growth hormone injection, but that hurdle will also be over soon. She has grown beautifully and is almost at a height within the realm of normalcy. (In fact, with my height at 5'2", I might be looking up to her soon, but then again, is that something new?)

Tovah still continues to be the devoted, loving sister to Rayna, and my pride for her grows every day. She's a teenager now, as Rayna is emerging into that stage as well. I love to watch Tovah fuss with Rayna's hair, lest she should have a "bad hair day," or talk to Rayna "about the boys." Their fights over who stirs the brownie mix may have been replaced with who gets the mirror first for their daily "primping" routines, as teenagers have been known to do, but they hold a bond that is truly deep, with a mutual respect for each other.

Allyn continues to approach Rayna's illness in the same way he has from the beginning: deep feelings inside, scientific, medical approach on the outside, with his guarded side, his inherent pessimism. Yet, this too has been slightly diminished in the miraculous results of Rayna's illness.

And me? I walk around with a new attitude, a new perspective, a more ethereal aura to my being, yet my defenses await armed and ready in the wings at all times. I take nothing for granted, never assume anything. I continue to revel in one of my all time favorite expressions in life.

"Motherhood? I wouldn't trade it for the world."

Oh, and one last thing: I still get wonderful hugs, two-handed ones.

Left to right: Tovah, Sandy, and Rayna